Managing Time and Stress

Other Books by Jeffrey L. Buller

Authentic Academic Leadership: A Values-Based Approach to College Administration

The Five Cultures of Academic Development: Crossing Boundaries in Higher Education Fundraising (with Dianne M. Reeves)

Hire the Right Faculty Member Every Time: Best Practices in Recruiting, Selecting, and Onboarding College Professors

Best Practices for Faculty Search Committees: How to Review Applications and Interview Candidates

Going for the Gold: How to Become a World-Class Academic Fundraiser (with Dianne M. Reeves)

World-Class Fundraising Isn't a Solo Sport: The Team Approach to Academic Fundraising (with Dianne M. Reeves)

A Toolkit for College Professors (with Robert E. Cipriano)

A Toolkit for Department Chairs (with Robert E. Cipriano)

Building Leadership Capacity: A Guide to Best Practices (with Walter H. Gmelch)

Change Leadership in Higher Education: A Practical Guide to Academic Transformation

Positive Academic Leadership: How to Stop Putting Out Fires and Start Making a Difference

Best Practices in Faculty Evaluation: A Practical Guide for Academic Leaders

Academic Leadership Day by Day: Small Steps That Lead to Great Success

The Essential Department Chair: A Comprehensive Desk Reference, Second Edition

The Essential Academic Dean: A Comprehensive Desk Reference, Second Edition

The Essential College Professor: A Practical Guide to an Academic Career

Managing Time and Stress

A Guide for Academic Leaders to Accomplish What Matters

Jeffrey L. Buller, PhD

ROWMAN & LITTLEFIELD
Lanham • Boulder • New York • London

Published by Rowman & Littlefield
A wholly owned subsidiary of the Rowman & Littlefield Publishing Group, Inc.
4501 Forbes Boulevard, Suite 200, Lanham, Maryland 20706
www.rowman.com

Unit A, Whitacre Mews, 26–34 Stannary Street, London SE11 4AB

Copyright © 2018 by Jeffrey L. Buller

All rights reserved. No part of this book may be reproduced in any form or by any electronic or mechanical means, including information storage and retrieval systems, without written permission from the publisher, except by a reviewer who may quote passages in a review.

British Library Cataloguing in Publication Information Available

Library of Congress Cataloging-in-Publication Data

Names: Buller, Jeffrey L., author.
Title: Managing Time and Stress : A Guide for Academic Leaders to Accomplish What Matters / Jeffrey L. Buller, PhD.
Description: Lanham, Maryland : Rowman & Littlefield, [2018] | Includes bibliographical references and index.
Identifiers: LCCN 2018027685 (print) | LCCN 2018040354 (ebook) | ISBN 9781475846003 (electronic) | ISBN 9781475845983 (cloth : alk. paper) | ISBN 9781475845990 (pbk. : alk. paper)
Subjects: LCSH: College administrators—Time management. | College administrators—Job stress. | Universities and colleges—Administration.
Classification: LCC LB2341 (ebook) | LCC LB2341 .B745 2018 (print) | DDC 378.1/01—dc23
LC record available at https://lccn.loc.gov/2018027685

To Walt Gmelch, Peter Seldin, Tim Hatfield, and Christian Hansen, my personal gurus in managing time and stress.

Contents

Introduction		ix
PART I: MANAGING YOUR TIME		**1**
1	Why Academic Leaders Need to Manage Their Time and Stress Better	3
2	Budgeting Time	7
3	Distinguishing the Urgent from the Important	13
4	The Time-Money Continuum	19
5	The Time-Energy Continuum	25
6	Time-Efficient Time Logs and How to Use Them	35
7	The Care and Feeding of To-Do Lists	41
8	Handling Documents Efficiently	47
9	Making SMART Goals Even SMARTER	55
10	Avoiding Black Holes of Time	61
11	Reprogramming Yourself	65
PART II: MANAGING YOUR STRESS		**71**
12	The Origins of Administrative Stress	73
13	Embracing Stress	83
14	Reducing Stress	93

15	Managing Stress	101
16	Coping with Stress	119

PART III: PUTTING IT ALL TOGETHER — **129**

17	A Holistic Approach to Managing Time and Stress	131
18	Academic Leaders as Role Models	139

Resources on Time and Stress Management for Academic Leaders	141
More about ATLAS	147
Index	151
About the Author	159

Introduction

Nearly every academic leadership workshop I've ever led on any topic eventually became a workshop on managing time and stress. We'd be talking about ways of improving communication within our units, building collegiality, developing creative plans for the future, or some other subject, and inevitably someone would say, "That's all well and good, but I barely have enough time to do the things I'm doing *now*," or "I'm under so much pressure from my dean (or provost, president, or board) that I can barely focus on what I need to do every day. I just can't handle taking on something new."

There's no doubt about it: Academic leaders today have too little time and are under more and more stress every year. And there's no doubt as to the reasons for this unfortunate state of affairs.

- Tighter academic budgets mean that academic leaders are often assigned more responsibilities this year than they were last year.
- The culture of accountability in higher education today puts them under constant pressure to demonstrate that their programs are growing and improving in quality at the same time that they're becoming increasingly cost-efficient.
- Many academic leaders seek to remain active as teachers and scholars at the same time they're serving as administrators, with the result that they feel they're trying to do two full-time jobs at once.
- Many students and their parents have come to view higher education as a commodity and can be unreasonably demanding of administrators that education be provided on the schedule they want at the cost they want with the results (a guaranteed degree leading to a guaranteed job) they want.
- New initiatives from state legislatures, institutional governing boards, and regional or discipline-specific accrediting agencies have increased the amount

of documentation academic leaders have to provide so as to verify that they're meeting performance standards (which often prove to be a moving target).
- Administrative supervisors, who may not be trained in how best to lead people within the distinctive organizational culture of higher education, may increase the stress of those who report to them by adopting management strategies better suited for the corporate or military worlds than the college or university.

Even on those occasions when academic leaders *do* seek help with managing their time or stress, they almost always focus on one of these topics to the exclusion of the other. They assume that, if they can get a handle on how to use their time better, their stress will automatically decrease or that if they were less distracted at work because of all the pressure they're under, they'd have plenty of time to get done everything they need to do. That approach usually doesn't work.

Managing time and stress has to go hand in hand. Even though perhaps the greatest cause of stress for academic leaders is insufficient time to do everything they need to do, time management is really only the first step toward becoming a more efficient and effective academic leader. They need to focus on time management first, but then adopt strategies to help them deal better with the stress inherent in their jobs. If they fail to do that, they'll soon slip back into patterns of poor time management by being so consumed by stress that they spend more time worrying about the work that needs to be done than they spend actually making progress.

The purpose of this book is to help you understand the processes that cause us to become inefficient and that lead to increased stress on the job and then to select a small set of strategies *that work for you* in managing your time and stress better. Every academic leader, in other words, needs a well-stocked toolkit of practical, rigorously tested approaches to use when to-do lists become too long and the amount of stress they face on the job threatens to overwhelm them.

You can think of this book, therefore, as sort of a "hardware store" from which you can select the specific "tools" you'll want in your individual "toolkit." Not every strategy will work for everyone, but I've tried to provide a large enough number that you should still be able to choose the best assortment that works for you.

You can use this book in a number of ways:

- If you've attended one of the workshops we offer at ATLAS Leadership Training on managing time and stress, this book can provide you a comprehensive set of notes outlining the ideas and strategies you explored there.
- If you're interested in studying on your own, this book provides a highly focused approach to the topic of managing time and stress within higher

education today. Unlike the management books on that you'll find in the business section of most bookstores, the examples you'll find in the pages that follow are all drawn from the world of higher education. You won't find yourself having to sort through a lot of advice that simply isn't practical for work at a college or university.
- If you're an academic leader who wants to help the people in your college, division, or department deal more effectively with managing time and stress, this work can be your textbook. It is designed to provide insights that are immediately practical, not merely theoretical, and to give you the instruments and examples you'll need in order to help others address the realities of academic life more effectively.

At the end of the work, you'll find an extensive list of resources on managing time and stress. Some of these materials are referred to in the text; others have been consulted as general references where appropriate. In either case, if you wish to continue exploring the issue of managing time and stress in an academic setting, the works cited in this list are an excellent place to begin.

In creating this book, I'd like to acknowledge the invaluable assistance of Rebecca Peter who provided editorial and research support at many stages of the project; Dana Babbs who created and provided permission to reproduce Figures 2.1, 2.2, and 12.1; Shiful Islam who created and provided permission to reproduce Figures 5.3, 5.4, and 15.1; K. V. (as he likes to be known) who created and provided permission to reproduce Figures 15.2, 15.3, 15.4, and 15.5; and PresenterMedia that gave me permission to reproduce Figures 5.1, 5.2, and 5.5.

I'd also like to thank Tom Koerner and Carlie Wall of Rowman & Littlefield who have been continually helpful and supportive during the creation of this book, as well as all the others they have helped me publish over the years. They have both helped me to manage my time well with little or no stress.

One final note: Although most parts of this book can be read in any order, when you start Part II, it's probably best to read chapter 12 ("The Origins of Administrative Stress") before skipping around to the other parts. In that chapter, certain vocabulary and concepts will be introduced, and there will be a number of inventories that you'll need to complete, all of which will be useful in the chapters that follow.

Except for that one proviso, I've tried to make the rest of this book as helpful, time-efficient, and (obviously) as stress-free as possible. So, the best thing to do is just to take a deep breath, relax, and plunge into chapter 1.

Jeffrey L. Buller
Jupiter, Florida
April 15, 2018

Part I

MANAGING YOUR TIME

Chapter 1

Why Academic Leaders Need to Manage Their Time and Stress Better

There's an old story about someone who invited a few friends over for dinner and was joined by them in the kitchen as he was preparing the meal. He took a roast out of the refrigerator and, before placing it into the oven, sliced about three inches off of each end and threw these pieces away. "Why did you do that?" one of his friends asked him. "I'm not sure," the man said, "but that's how my mother always did it, and she was a really good cook."

The next time the man was at his mother's house, they happened to be having a roast, and, once again, she sliced about three inches off of each end and threw both pieces away. "Why do you do that whenever you make a roast," the man asked. "I'm not entirely sure. But that's the way my mother always did it, and she was a really good cook." The question puzzled them enough that they decided to call the man's grandmother and find out.

"Grandma," the man said when he got her on the phone, "why, when you're making a roast, do you always cut three inches off of both ends and throw them away?" The older woman didn't pause a second, "Well, you see, dear, my roasting pan is just so small."

Many of our practices as academic leaders are much like that family's approach to cooking a roast: We do things in the way we've always done them or because that's how we've seen other people do them, but the end result is wasteful and stressful. And as academic leaders today, we have precious little time to waste and far too much stress as it is without adding any more unnecessarily.

The workload of the typical department chair, dean, provost, or president is increasing dramatically. Tight budgets mean that we have to devote more of our efforts to fund-raising and grant writing. Competition for students means that we can no longer assume that it's the job of the admissions office to recruit students and our job to teach them; regardless of our titles, we're all student recruiters now.

The necessity to be accountable for what we do has greatly expanded the demands on us for outcome assessment, program review, and participation in accreditation processes for our programs. Declines in civility and increasing student expectations for services often make us feel that we could spend our days doing nothing else but dealing with conflicts, complaints, and demands by stakeholders to be heard. Time management isn't a luxury for academic leaders; it's a critical skill for them to be able to do their jobs effectively.

But the truth of the matter is that relatively few of us are very good at managing time and stress. Trained as researchers, we expect that when we get faculty positions, we'll do pretty much the same things we were doing as graduate students and just find time to fit in the additional teaching, publication, and committee work that's now required of us.

Then, if we're successful in doing that, we become deans and chairs, expecting to do pretty much the same things we were doing as professors and just finding time to fit in the extra meetings, evaluations, reports, and all the rest of the duties that come to us as administrators. In essence, we become really good at adding responsibilities to our loads but not very good at:

- subtracting tasks that are no longer productive or necessary;
- multiplying the number of people around us with leadership skills so that we don't have to do everything ourselves;
- dividing our responsibilities and delegating appropriate ones to others so that we can focus on our highest priorities.

Moreover, as we'll see later, the organizational culture of the typical college or university often seems to be an obstacle to efficiency and stress reduction. In a typical hierarchy, decisions can be passed down the chain from the top of the organization to the bottom relatively quickly, and even major strategic changes can be implemented in very little time. But in higher education, where so much is done through committee structures and dependent on policies that are often not even set at the local level, doing a relatively simple task can take months. And that's a very stressful environment in which to work.

What exacerbates this problem is that we don't have that many months available each year for us to achieve our highest priorities. Many faculty members aren't around in the summer. A month at the beginning of each academic year is spent in starting projects back up again. Later in the term, significant time is needed for final exams, and then there's winter break.

A spring semester can often feel as though the year is starting all over again, but then time has to be allocated to spring break, and, a short time later, it seems as though we're preparing for commencement. The standard academic "year" is really a matter of perhaps fifteen or twenty truly productive *weeks*, with all kinds of priorities vying for our attention during this limited period.

A great deal of what we need to do in managing time and stress, therefore, is really just a function of good academic leadership. It involves understanding what our jobs are now—not what they were back when we were faculty members or held different administrative positions—and focusing our attention on those tasks that are most important to the success of our programs. Learning to be an academic leader is a bit too broad a topic for a single book; it basically encompasses everything that you might be learning at leadership development seminars, through webinars, via professional journals, in books, and in all the other formats it uses to convey skills and knowledge to academic leaders. But what this book *can* do is improve your skills at managing time and stress by helping you:

- use time more effectively so that you're more likely to achieve the results you want;
- adopt a few simple tools and processes that can make a big difference in your efficiency and productivity;
- understand how you spend your time;
- stop viewing stress as an impediment and start viewing it as a natural part of your job;
- reduce your stress both by managing your time better and by finding ways to relax during periods of intense pressure.

Of these five goals, the one that may have surprised you was the notion that we want to engage in a systematic exploration of how you spend your time. After all, you probably already think you have a pretty good handle on how you spend your time: "Meetings, pointless meetings, more meetings, mind-numbing paperwork, and then . . . oh, yes, still more meetings." When we're being cynical (or realistic, depending on your perspective) that's largely how we view the bane of the administrator's existence: meetings and paperwork.

If you happen to be in a position where you can cut down on the number of meetings people have to attend and the forms they need to complete, it's an excellent use of your authority to do so. You'll be managing other people's time better as well as your own.

But what if you can't control how many meetings you have and how many reports you are required to submit? And what about those other activities that also consume an administrator's day: dealing with personnel issues? How do you handle those more efficiently and in ways that cause you less anxiety and stress?

There are actually research-proven and field-tested ways to achieve all the goals listed earlier, even if you can't control every aspect of your schedule. The very first method that we'll consider introduces us to a key principle of effective time management that we'll have occasion to return to many times: *We have to learn how to budget our time more successfully so that we can invest our time more strategically.* And that is the principle that we'll begin exploring in the next chapter.

Chapter 2

Budgeting Time

Time is only one of the resources we are required to manage as academic leaders. We also have to manage such things as money, equipment, the faculty and staff we work with, the flow of information that we want to make available to others, the buildings we use for teaching and research, and plenty more as well (Hansen, 2011, 22–29). For the ease of illustration, let's focus on just two of these: time and money. Which of the two do you find easier to manage?

When I ask this question in my workshops, usually about two-thirds to three-quarters of the people say that they find it easier to manage money rather than time. From one perspective, that's not at all surprising: They're attending a time management workshop, after all, and people who believe their time management skills are excellent tend not to enroll in these programs. But from another perspective, *most* people find money easier to manage than time. If you end up wasting money, you still have options. You can always make more money. And if you wasted money on a defective good or poor service, there's the possibility of a refund.

But time isn't like that. Once it's gone, it's gone forever. So, let's conduct a little experiment. I call it the *Brewster's Million's Experiment* because it was inspired by the Richard Pryor comedy *Brewster's Millions* (1985). In that movie, a minor league ballplayer, Montgomery Brewster, learns that his great uncle has left him a substantial amount of money in a will.

But there are some terms Brewster has to meet in order to receive the inheritance. He has to spend $30 million in thirty days under very strict conditions:

- At the end of the thirty days, he can't own any assets.
- He can hire people, but he has to get value for their services.
- He can donate 5 percent, and he can lose 5 percent gambling, but he can't just give the money away or spend it on presents for others.

- He can't destroy anything of value that he buys.
- He can't tell anyone why he is spending this money.

Under those conditions, even though Brewster has a lot of money available, it becomes difficult to manage it in a way where he can spend it all in the time allowed.

In our experiment, we're going to try to do something similar. We're going to imagine that a local bank is holding a contest. If you can figure out a way to spend *exactly* $604,800 in one week, you get to keep everything you purchase. If you cannot spend exactly that amount, you get nothing. But there are a number of very strict rules that you have to follow:

- You may use the money on goods, services, or any combination of the two.
- Unlike Montgomery Brewster, you may not give away any of the money. (That would make it too easy: You could simply donate any money that was left after you spent as much as you could.)
- You must purchase at least five different goods or services. You can purchase more if you like, but you cannot purchase fewer than five.
- You must verify prices against a vendor or service provider who lists the cost of that precise item online.
- Cents count. You may not simply round things off to the nearest dollar.

Conduct the exercise, and see how close you can get to spending exactly $604,800. Your first few choices are likely to be the easiest. It's when you get down to those last few dollars and cents that you really have to become creative. But remember: According to the terms of the contest, you wouldn't get *anything* unless you spent every last bit of the money allocated. So, be as creative as you can in figuring out ways to use the money.

Then, once you've found a way to spend exactly $604,800, do the following:

- Go through your list of expenditures and group them into categories to determine *what* you spent the money on. In other words, what were your big priorities? Housing? Items that you need for your job? Services to make your life (or the lives of your loved ones) a little easier? Gifts? Travel? Perhaps a few luxuries you couldn't afford otherwise? As you look at your list in this way, you'll gain insight into what your *priorities* are.
- Next, consider *how* you went about spending the money. Where did you begin? Did you start by allocating funds for your biggest priority or greatest need? Was the first purchase that came to your mind a luxury item because the contest represented "found money" and enables you to splurge a bit? Was your first impulse to pay off the mortgage and other outstanding bills

so that your future would be more secure? What was the process you used to select the items on that list, and what values or general principles does that process represent?
- How easy did you find this exercise? Was budgeting money (even imaginary money) as easy as you had expected? Do you think it would've been easier if the exercise had involved managing time?
- Finally, review how you spent the last few dollars and cents that you had available. Were you looking only for items with a price that happened to match the amount that you had available? Or did your priorities still come into play? In other words, when the money started getting tight, did you waste it (spending it just to spend it) or invest it (spending it on less expensive goods and services that still reflect your priorities)?

The point of this exercise is to offer you some perspective on your current approaches to matters of budget and management. Now that you've clarified your priorities, we can use them to help you manage your time more effectively.

And there's also one more insight we can gain from this exercise. Consider the following:

- There are 60 seconds in a minute.
- There are 60 minutes (3,600 seconds) in an hour.
- There are 24 hours (86,400 seconds) in a day.
- And there are 7 days (604,800 seconds) in a week.

In other words, every week you have exactly the same number of seconds to "budget" as you had dollars to budget in our exercise. That's why that last reflection—how did you spend the remaining money when there were only a few dollars and cents left?—becomes so important.

People often manage their time in the same way as their money. When only a little bit of time is left, they waste it, assuming that they don't have enough time to do anything meaningful. But those little bits of remaining time are important: If we "spend" them wisely by investing them in activities that are significant, we're less likely to run out of time when we really need it.

In short, you can budget your time in much the same way that you budgeted your money in the exercise. So, as you think about budgeting time for your week (or month, semester, or year), use the same process that we explored in the Brewster's Millions Experiment, but apply the lessons you drew from conducting that experiment:

- Base your "time budget" on your priorities. What are the most important things you have to accomplish during the period you're planning for? In

order to accomplish those priorities, when would you need to begin each activity? What markers of timely progress would you need to set along the way?
- Don't waste the little bits and pieces of time that are left after you construct your plan. Just as it was probably a challenge to spend the last few bits of the imaginary $604,800 in our experiment, you're likely to have a few random hours and minutes left over after you block out time for the important activities in your schedule. How people spend those small bits of time is what distinguishes time wasters from effective time managers. If you have only 43 minutes of work time left in your schedule as you prepare your week's plan, you may not think that you have enough time left to do anything significant like write a grant proposal or revise your syllabus. But it *is* enough time to write a paragraph or two for that grant proposal or rewrite your statement of expectations in your syllabus. It would also be enough time to complete those other activities you may have been putting off, like writing a letter of recommendation or returning someone's phone call. Combined effectively, these little "time puddles" eventually build to become vast "time lakes," and you discover that you've had more time at your disposal than you previously thought.

ROCKS, PEBBLES, AND SAND

An interesting thing happens if you give people a number of large items (like rocks), medium-sized items (like pebbles), and small items (like sand) and ask them to try fitting them all into a container. Most people will put the sand in first, on the assumption that it's going to sift to the bottom anyway, then put the pebbles in, and finally try to put the rocks in. But if they do that, they find that it doesn't all fit. They end up with a number of rocks that are too large for the container, as illustrated in Figure 2.1.

In order to make it all fit, you have to put the rocks in first, shake the container so that they fit into the tightest amount of space possible, then put the pebbles in, shake the container again so that the pebbles fill in the space between the rocks, finally pour in the sand, and shake the container one more time so that the sand fills in the space between the pebbles. If you do that, you end up with everything inside the container, as illustrated in Figure 2.2.

The rocks, pebbles, and sand in this illustration are metaphors for how we should construct our time budget. The rocks are the really important things we have to do. The pebbles are the things that have at least some importance. And the sand represents minor, insignificant activities. Most people spend a great deal of their day in activities that aren't particularly important. That probably leaves them enough time to do the things that have at least some

Figure 2.1

Figure 2.2

importance, but when they come to the truly significant activities—the ones that have an impact both on their careers and on the quality of their programs—they run out of time.

The way in which we budget our time most effectively is to put in the "rocks" first: Block out time for the truly significant goals we want to accomplish. The activities that have at least some importance can be scheduled around those, and everything else tends to fit into the "cracks" and "pockets" that then remain in our schedules. As a first step in effective time management, therefore, draw up a list of at least three but no more than twelve goals or activities that you regard as most important to you professionally. These should be objectives that reflect why you became an academic leader and what you hope to accomplish in your position.

Of course, even the list of goals or activities you just created may be too long for you to use it in scheduling your actual workday. That's why, once you've decided on your list of major objectives, it's time to go on to the second strategy that we'll consider: distinguishing what's urgent from what's important.

Chapter 3

Distinguishing the Urgent from the Important

Dwight D. Eisenhower, supreme commander of the Allied Expeditionary Forces in Europe and later president of the United States, was fond of saying, "What is important is seldom urgent, and what is urgent is seldom important." At first, such a statement appears almost Zen-like in its obscurity. After all, aren't the words *urgent* and *important* synonyms? Isn't Eisenhower's observation a bit like saying, "Fall is seldom autumn, and autumn is seldom fall"?

In fact, there is indeed an important distinction between what's important and what's urgent. Things are important because they *matter*; things are urgent because they have to be *done immediately* (table 3.1). What Eisenhower was saying is that simply because something has a tight deadline that doesn't mean that it deserves our greatest attention. To put it in modern terms, *your e-mail inbox shouldn't define your goals for the day.*

That is to say, something becomes urgent for us if its deadline is staring us right in the face. Usually those deadlines are imposed on us by someone else, and so our primary concern becomes avoiding failure by not missing the deadlines.

Table 3.1 Urgent versus Important

Urgent	Important
schedule driven	impact-driven
externally driven	internally driven
fundamentally negative, focusing on "What happens if I fail?"	fundamentally positive, focusing on "What happens if I succeed?"

Something that's important is going to have significant impact. It'll matter to us months, perhaps even years, from now. It's internally driven by who we are, what our core values are, and where we want our careers and programs to go in the future. It is based on a positive vision of the benefits that might develop if only we can achieve this critical goal.

Stephen R. Covey's third habit in his *Seven Habits of Highly Effective People* (1989) is to *Put First Things First*, and he combines Eisenhower's binary distinction between the urgent and important into a four-category system, as shown in Table 3.2.

If you had tasks to complete that fell into these various quadrants, you'd know better than to begin with the items that fall into Quadrant 4. Everyone knows that the place to begin with is Quadrant 1. But the mistake most people make is that, after giving their attention to the tasks that are both urgent and important, they give their next priority to the items that are urgent but not all that important. After all, there's that deadline coming up, and they've got to meet it!

Thinking in that way is a time management trap. It means that we tend to overlook important activities—the very tasks that can make our programs better and advance our careers—simply because they don't have immediate deadlines. That's why so many faculty members get a great deal of research accomplished until they get tenure and become less productive. The urgency of the tenure clock drives them in a way that the importance of their research doesn't once; there's no pressing deadline on their calendars.

The key to time management is to deal with the urgent and important first but then to give due attention to the things that are important even if they're not particularly urgent. If you do that, Quadrants 1 and 2 (the categories that include what's important) begin to occupy more and more of your workday than do Quadrants 3 and 4 (the categories that don't include what's important). And that's good time management: You're spending your day doing what really matters.

Of course, colleges and universities vary a great deal in terms of how they treat deadlines. At certain schools, deadlines are regarded as very strict. A promotion application due at 5:00 p.m. will be automatically rejected if you try to turn it in at 5:03 p.m. And if you're applying for an externally funded grant,

Table 3.2 The Four Quadrants

Quadrant 1: Things that are both urgent and important.	Quadrant 2: Things that are important but not urgent.
Quadrant 3: Things that are urgent but not important.	Quadrant 4: Things that are neither urgent nor important.

Source: Covey (1989, 154–192).

you have to be absolutely scrupulous about meeting the funding agency's deadline.

In most cases, however, academic leaders learn that *most internally imposed deadlines at colleges and universities are more flexible than they may initially appear*. It depends on the personality of your supervisor, but, in most cases, getting a report a day or two late doesn't result in serious consequences.

That's not an excuse for procrastination, but it does mean that if you have only a limited amount of time available and have to choose between something that will truly matter to your program or career and something that has a tight deadline but consists of routine paperwork, you're probably better off spending your time on the activity that's really going to make a difference.

In addition, distinguishing the urgent from the important is sometimes a personal decision. How you categorize an activity may differ from how one of your colleagues who has different priorities, perspectives, and values does. So, as an exercise in exploring your own approach to what's important and what's urgent, we'll conduct a short thought experiment.

Imagine that you've collected all the tasks that you can engage in over the next week or so and want to figure out how best to allocate your time. Assign each of the following activities to one of Covey's four quadrants using Table 3.2 for reference. Write the number of one of these quadrants in front of each activity, based on the degrees of urgency and importance you would attribute to that activity.

_____ A. Learning a new language
_____ B. Updating your Facebook status
_____ C. Returning a call from your supervisor
_____ D. Attending a campus workshop on academic leadership
_____ E. Going to an intercollegiate athletic event in your school's most popular sport
_____ F. Checking for new e-mail
_____ G. A routine dental appointment
_____ H. Having the oil changed in your car
_____ I. Spending time with your family
_____ J. Reading for pleasure
_____ K. Preparing a course you'll teach a year from now (or, if you don't teach, preparing a major new proposal that you'll present to a committee a year from now)
_____ L. Returning a call from the college/university president/chancellor
_____ M. Responding to a survey from a professional organization about your stress level

_____ N. Reading the minutes of the faculty or staff senate (or an equivalent body at your institution)
_____ O. Completing a grant application that is due in a week
_____ P. Finishing your annual report of activities that's due in three months
_____ Q. Helping a friend move
_____ R. Returning a library book that's due today
_____ S. Reading professional articles related to your position or specialty
_____ T. Sending a thank-you note to a mentor who recommended you for a great opportunity
_____ U. Cleaning your office and getting rid of unneeded papers
_____ V. Working on a grant application that is due in six months
_____ W. Meeting colleagues from other offices or disciplines at your institution
_____ X. Holding an initial meeting to get acquainted with a prospective donor
_____ Y. Representing your office or program at a recruiting event for prospective students
_____ Z. Attending a national academic leadership training program seminar on a topic closely related to the responsibilities you have in your position

Once you've completed this inventory, review your answers, and see if you've assigned too many to the same quadrant. If more than seven activities are listed as falling into Quadrant 1, you may not have been meticulous enough in distinguishing the urgent from the important. Go through these Quadrant 1 activities and reclassify some of them as Quadrant 2 or Quadrant 3 until you have no more than seven items assigned to Quadrant 1. Then go through the other quadrants to make sure that you've given careful thought to exactly how urgent and important you regard each of the activities you've placed in each category.

When you're completely satisfied with your results, review the list once again to determine whether you can find any consistent patterns. For example, do the activities you classified as important tend to relate to your personal or professional success, the quality of your program, or something else? What do you notice about the activities you characterized as neither urgent nor important? What does that insight tell you about actual activities that you may want to remove from your schedule or allocate less time for?

By removing certain activities from your schedule or reducing the amount of time you're willing to devote to them, you've made genuine progress in time management. You've recovered some time that would have been devoted to activities that would have been time-consuming without producing much benefit to you or your program.

You now have an opportunity to schedule in more of the "rocks" and even a few of the "pebbles" that we discussed in chapter 2. Block out time for the activities that will really matter to you, even if they don't have an immediate deadline. By doing so, you'll discover that you've redirected your energy toward activities that will make you much more efficient and productive both in your own eyes and in the opinions of your supervisor and key stakeholders.

Chapter 4

The Time-Money Continuum

Albert Einstein is famous for his concept of the space-time continuum: the notion that space and time are not really separate phenomena but can merge into one another. In time management, we want to consider a parallel phenomenon: the Time-Money Continuum, the notion that, as we saw with the Brewster's Millions Experiment, there are ways in which time can be seen as money and money can be seen as time.

The Time-Money Continuum works this way: There are certain activities that require an investment of significant time but not much money that we could also perform by investing more money but not much time. Imagine that a window breaks at your house and that you're not particularly skilled at home repairs. You can either devote the better part of a day getting the parts you need and repairing the window yourself (large time investment, small monetary investment) or hire someone to do the job for you (small time investment, large monetary investment).

We make this kind of trade-off between time and money constantly: preparing your taxes yourself or paying someone to do them, cleaning your home or hiring a housekeeper, washing your car at home or taking it to the car wash, and so on. But we also sometimes get trapped into investing time in an activity rather than money because we've always done that job ourselves or because we overestimate how much it would cost to have someone perform the task for us.

It may make sense early in our careers to repair the window, prepare our taxes, clean our houses, and wash our cars ourselves because we have a lot of time then and not much money. But as our situations change, it may not make sense to continue doing so when our income has increased and we have less time. *Time becomes more valuable than money.*

That last phrase is the key: Time and money are resources, and the goal of good resource management is always to *spend the least valuable resource necessary to accomplish any given task.* In our work as academic leaders, time and money are only two of the resources that we have available to us.

- We also have *people resources*. There are people who work in our areas to whom we can delegate certain responsibilities. They benefit by gaining professional experience. We benefit by having more time available to us for other important goals.
- We have *information resources*. If we already know something, we don't have to spend the time investigating it.
- We have *technology resources*. If "there's an app for that," our phones, tablets, and computers can perform tasks much more quickly (and usually with greater accuracy) than we can perform the tasks ourselves.
- We have *communication resources*. If we can handle a meeting through a phone call or video conference, we can save the travel time it would have required to conduct a face-to-face meeting.
- We have *space resources*. If our offices are arranged more efficiently, we don't waste time looking for misplaced documents or having to walk across the room to use something that could have been within our reach to begin with.

In short, we don't really have just a Time-Money Continuum but a huge nexus of time, money, people, information, technology, communication, and space to draw from, as illustrated in Figure 4.1.

And our goal should always be to spend whichever of these resources is least valuable or expensive to us at the time.

If we're working in an office with administrative support staff and this time of year is one when people are not already overworked because of all the tasks assigned to them, people resources may be our least "valuable" or "expensive" resource at the moment. But if everyone is already far overcommitted, outsourcing a few tasks may make better sense because money is then our least "valuable" or "expensive" resource.

Understanding that we have a full nexus of resources available to us can make us far more effective in managing our time.

- It means that we might hire a student worker every now and then to straighten up our offices. By doing so, we improve our space resources by making it easier for us to find things and free ourselves up to devote our attention to activities that will have a great impact on our program or career. We also provide additional income to someone for whom money is probably the most valuable resource at the moment.

The Time-Money Continuum

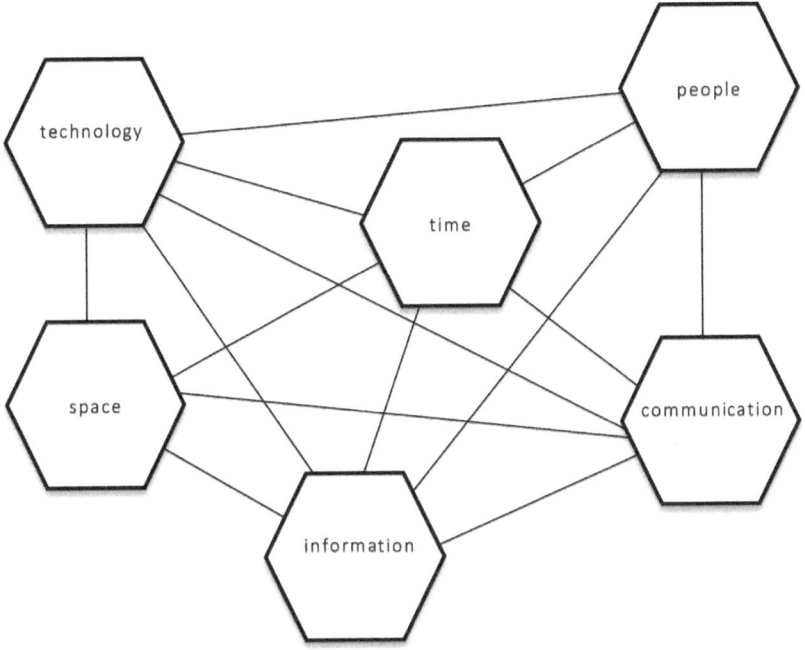

Figure 4.1

- It means that we might engage in conference calls while traveling to a meeting that must be conducted face-to-face. By doing so, we use our communication resources to further reduce time that would have to be spent traveling and avoid wasting the time that we may have spent accomplishing nothing more than getting from one place to another.
- It means that we might have an administrative assistant proofread and edit our memos and scholarly articles. By doing so, we rely on our people resources to free ourselves up to draft other memos and articles, thus increasing our overall productivity.

The availability of services through the Internet means that a great deal of time can be saved with a relatively small investment of money. A search on the key words *virtual assistance* will provide you with websites for a number of services and private contractors who can arrange your travel, respond to routine e-mail messages, schedule your appointments, initiate presentations in PowerPoint or Keynote, create forms, conduct basic research, edit audio or video files, perform basic copywriting, develop or improve a website, translate text from one language to another, design a logo, or accomplish dozens of other tasks.

Some of these sites, such as Fiverr (www.fiverr.com), allow various freelancers to bid for jobs you post, while others such as UpWork (www.upwork.com) allow you to commission professionals on an hourly basis. Still other services, such as TaskRabbit (www.taskrabbit.com) put you in contact with local people who can run errands for you, install or assemble basic equipment and furniture, perform yard work, or help you pack for a move. In this way, you can devote your time and attention to the sorts of activities where your expertise is actually needed and outsource tasks that would merely occupy your time and cause you stress.

In creating this book, for example, Figures 2.1, 2.2, and 12.1 were created by a professional graphic designer, Figures 5.1, 5.2, and 5.5 were used with permission from a professional graphic design service, Figures 5.4, 5.3, 15.1, 15.2, 15.3, 15.4, and 15.5 were provided in response to several requests that I posted on Fiverr, and Figures 4.1 and 17.1 were created by the author's use of the graphics features of Microsoft Word.

You can decide for yourself whether the additional cost of hiring a graphic designer or subscribing to a graphic design service is worth the added expense of posting requests on a website like Fiverr. From my own perspective, however, if I had tried to do all that work myself—not to mention the hours required to proofread, edit, and format my rough draft which was done by my editorial assistant—the book would have taken far longer to complete, and the result would have been of lower quality. So, to my mind, outsourcing the right tasks simply makes sense.

You can also make better use of time by taking a train to a meeting that you'd ordinarily drive to and working (or even relaxing) instead of staring through your windshield and fighting road rage. On those occasions when you do have to drive, consider listening to an audiobook of a work on improving leadership—or perhaps stress or time management!—to make the best possible use of your hours on the road. And although it may seem extravagant, hiring a driver or car service to get you where you need to go can free you up to review documents, make phone calls, and perform other tasks while someone else is negotiating the traffic in the city or on the interstate.

Just remember that many of these services are ones that you'll have to pay for yourself. Your college or university may balk at reimbursing you for a personal driver and may even hesitate to pick up the cost of outsourcing a PowerPoint presentation. But even though these expenditures are your own, they'll be worth it to you if your time is more valuable to you than the investment of money involved.

To take full advantage of the Time-Money Continuum or Nexus of Resources, start by completing the list that appears in Table 4.1. In the left column, identify a time-intensive task that you don't particularly enjoy doing or that doesn't seem worth the time it takes for you to accomplish it.

In the center column, state whether that task can legitimately be outsourced. For example, you can reasonably outsource the development of a spreadsheet that automatically averages and calculates student grades according to the weights assigned in your syllabus. You can't legitimately outsource attending the weekly one-on-one meetings with your boss that always seem to require more time than they're worth.

If the task can be outsourced, enter a figure in the right column that indicates the highest you'd be willing to pay someone to perform that task. For example, suppose you have a presentation to give at an upcoming conference, and you really hate the mundane task of converting your written paper into a PowerPoint or Keynote presentation for use at the conference. It always takes you far too long to develop these presentations, you don't find the work gratifying, and you don't think that you're particularly good at it.

Could you outsource the task? You certainly can. You're not asking anyone to conduct scholarly research for which you'll take credit. You've already done the research; you merely want the presentation formatted in an attractive manner. How much would you be willing to pay someone to perform this task? That answer is really up to you. You might find a student willing to draft a basic version for you that costs only $10. But for $250, you might find an independent contractor who can construct a truly elegant presentation. The price point you select is merely a reflection of how much it's worth it to you to have someone else perform that task.

Once you've identified the tasks that can be outsourced and the price you're willing to pay for them, you can begin to identify campus workers or

Table 4.1 The Time-Money Continuum or Nexus of Resources

Time-Intensive Task	Can It Be Outsourced?	Dollar Value to You

online sites that will perform the task at the price you're willing to pay. The people you hire will be happy because you're providing them with income. You'll be happy because you'll have freed yourself of an unpleasant task and now have more time to devote to more important or enjoyable activities.

What you are actually doing when you complete Table 4.1 is calculating one aspect of the *opportunity cost* of various activities. Everything we do has both an actual cost and an opportunity cost. For example, if you go to a movie, the actual cost would reflect the price of admission plus the price of any snacks you purchase to consume during the movie. But the opportunity cost would reflect what you could have been doing if you hadn't attended the movie in the first place. Maybe you could have given a presentation for a local group that would have paid you an honorarium. In that case, the total cost of the movie would have been the actual cost of what you paid out of pocket *plus* the amount of the honorarium that you didn't receive. Seen from this perspective, the movie could turn out to have been a very expensive afternoon indeed!

But there's also a positive side to opportunity costs. You might enjoy conducting research and writing the first drafts of articles or books but hate the polishing, proofreading, and formatting required to get your work into print. In that case, doing the work that you enjoy and then hiring a copy editor to perform the tasks that you find less appealing is simply a smart way of using your nexus of resources. While the copy editor is preparing your first publication, you can devote your attention to the aspects you enjoy on your second publication, doubling your productivity and eliminating the stress you may have had from doing work you don't like. You simply have to calculate at what point the opportunity costs required to perform the task yourself are greater than the financial costs of outsourcing it to make the best use of the limited time that you have available.

Chapter 5

The Time-Energy Continuum

In the last chapter, we saw that time was only one part of a nexus of resources (including people, technology, information, communication, and space) that academic leaders have available to them. Now we want to add one additional component to that list of resources: energy.

Each of us has his or her own personal energy cycle. Some of us are morning people and get more done before noon than others get done all day. Others are night owls and tend to be at their most productive when others have gone to bed. Knowing your personal energy cycle can help you synchronize your work—and even more important, the *type* of work that you do—to the time of day when you're most likely to be efficient at that particular task (Loehr and Schwartz, 2005; Dore, 2017).

The distinction between morning people and night owls that we just considered is probably something you've already thought about. But there are several variations within these common patterns that academic leaders often overlook to the detriment of their productivity and ability to manage their time well. Sometimes these energy patterns are referred to as *Circadian Rhythms* or *Ultradian Rhythms*, the internal "body clocks" that each of us has (Jonat, 2014). Circadian rhythms refer to cycles over the course of about a 24-hour period. Ultradian rhythms refer to cycles of about 90 to 120 minutes.

Although everyone functions under both circadian and ultradian rhythms, some people's mental energies, specifically, may align more so with one rather than the other, and these patterns vary significantly from person to person, including among you and your coworkers. Examples of some circadian "types" include the battery, the skier, and the plateau, whereas ultradian "types" include the camel and the trampoline. Let's explore each of these types in more detail.

We may think of some people and their energy cycles as *batteries* (see Figure 5.1). In the morning, beginning shortly after they wake up, their energy level is the highest that it will be all day. For the rest of the day, their energy drains steadily until they have very little stamina for serious work in the late afternoon or evening.

We can regard other people as *skiers* due to their cycles (see Figure 5.2). It takes them a little time to get started each day but about midmorning they

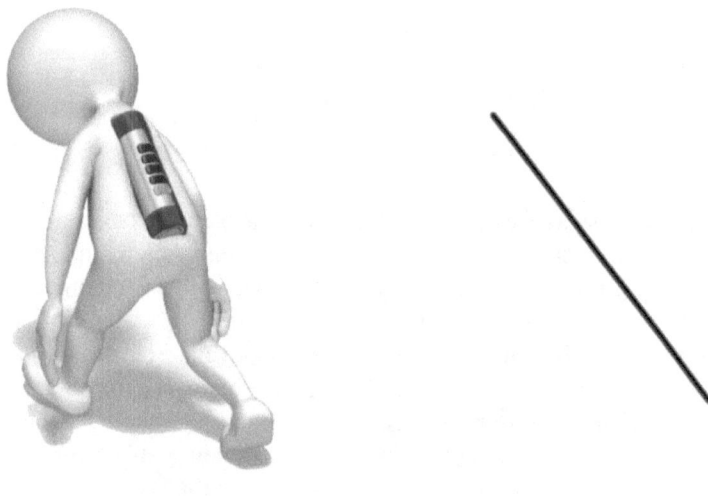

Figure 5.1

Figure 5.2

reach their energy peak, after which their pattern is rather similar to that of batteries: Their energy drains progressively throughout the rest of the day.

Plateaus (see Figure 5.3) build to one, extended energy peak. They may be able to maintain their periods of high energy for five or six hours a day. But once their energy is consumed, their feeling of decline can be rather sudden, and they have no additional periods of high energy that day.

Another common energy cycle type is the *Bactrian camel* (see Figure 5.4). Unlike their more familiar dromedary relatives, Bactrian camels have two humps, and people who have this energy cycle have two periods of peak energy each day with a slump in between. For example, they may find that they are alert in the mid- to late morning, experience a lull in the afternoon, and have a "second wind" in the evening.

Finally, *trampolines* (see Figure 5.5) are a little like Bactrian camels—they have more than one period of high energy each day, with slumps separating these more alert phases—except that their peak energy periods number more than two. They may have three, four, or even five times during the day when they feel particularly alert and capable of handling their most challenging work.

Figure 5.3

Figure 5.4

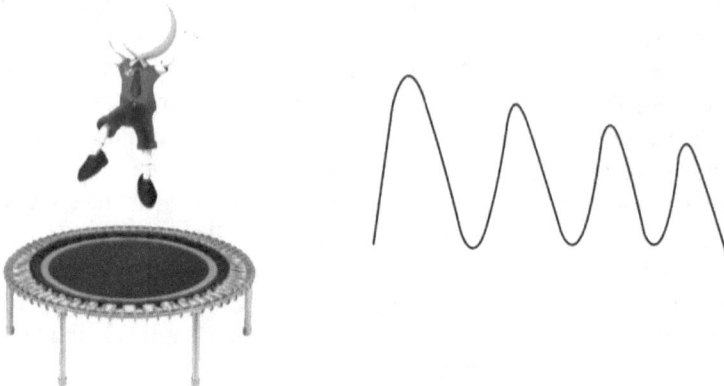

Figure 5.5

But the number of these high energy cycles varies from person to person and sometimes even from day to day. Also, like someone who leaps onto a trampoline and lets inertia control how high he or she bounces, their first energy peak is generally the highest, with each successive peak slightly lower than the one before.

These five energy patterns are not the only ones that exist, but they are the most common. As you reflect on how your energy tends to rise and fall during the day, which of these patterns seems to fit you the best? Or, if none of the patterns listed here seems quite right, how would you describe or graph your own personal energy cycle?

Understanding your personal energy cycle is useful because of the next important principle of time management that we want to consider: *Sometimes being more productive isn't just about selecting the right priorities; it's also about matching those priorities to the best times in your energy cycle.*

Certainly, you can't control every aspect of your energy cycle. If you have a boss who insists on scheduling long, dull meetings during the morning, which happens to be your most productive time of day, you could suggest that the meeting time be changed, but you can't really insist. In addition, it's always possible that your boss scheduled those meetings for the best time in his or her own energy cycle. Our own daily rhythms don't always synchronize with those of our supervisors and stakeholders.

Nevertheless, to the extent that you *do* control your schedule, linking those activities that require the greatest energy to the periods of your day when you're most alert can greatly increase your skills at time management. Let's consider how you might match what you do as an academic leader to the best times of the day for you to do each activity. Table 5.1 is a list of some of the

Table 5.1 Linking Energy to Activities

- A. I perform this activity best when I have a very high level of energy.
- B. I can perform this activity effectively with a moderate amount of energy.
- C. I can perform this activity effectively with a relatively low amount of energy.
- D. I can perform this activity effectively with almost no energy at all. It's the sort of thing about which I might say, "I could do this in my sleep."
- E. I do not ever perform this activity.

____ 1. Delegating responsibilities to others
____ 2. Attending meetings where my supervisor is present
____ 3. Attending meetings where I am in charge
____ 4. Attending meetings where I am not in charge and my supervisor is not present
____ 5. Developing plans and setting long-term goals for my program
____ 6. Reading and responding to e-mail
____ 7. Sorting through and acting on traditional "paper mail" and memos
____ 8. Planning budgets
____ 9. Implementing, supervising, or budgeting
____10. Evaluating members of the faculty
____11. Evaluating members of the staff
____12. Preparing for the courses I teach
____13. Teaching courses
____14. Grading assignments, tests, and papers from the courses I teach
____15. Meeting with an advisory or governing board
____16. Developing a vision for my program or the institution
____17. Engaging in activities related to outcomes assessment
____18. Engaging in program review
____19. Engaging in accreditation activities
____20. "Managing by walking around"; providing informal supervision of my area
____21. Meeting with potential donors
____22. Writing grant proposals
____23. Performing research by collecting data or gathering information
____24. Interpreting the data or information from my research
____25. Writing up my research results
____26. Advocating on behalf of my area or institution with supervisors or board members
____27. Advocating on behalf of my area or institution with members of the administration
____28. Discussing performance problems with faculty members
____29. Discussing performance problems with staff members
____30. Discussing performance problems with students
____31. General or routine committee work
____32. Interviewing prospective faculty members
____33. Interviewing prospective staff members
____34. Recruiting prospective students
____35. Making offers to and negotiating compensation with prospective members of the faculty or staff
____36. Notifying members of the faculty or staff that they are terminated or that their contracts are not being renewed

tasks commonly performed by academic leaders. Read the list, and, then, in the space before each activity, enter one of the following selections.

Since every academic leadership position is different, there is likely to be a number of activities important to your work that are not represented on this list. Feel free to add them and then to identify the energy level you need in order to perform them effectively. Then ask yourself the following questions:

- Do I generally perform this activity at the point in my energy cycle that is most suitable?
- Do I have any control over that timing?

You may discover that you're not getting as much done as you like, not because you have too much to do, but because you're trying to do things at the wrong time of the day. For example, when academic leaders have to terminate members of the faculty or staff or notify them that their contracts are not being renewed, they generally schedule these activities for late in the day. The assumption is that the employee can then go home and deal with his or her disappointment in private. And from the perspective of compassion, that may indeed be the best time of day for this task.

But if you've discovered that the end of the day is when your energy level is the lowest and so you end up saying the wrong things in these conversations or reply poorly when challenged, then your feelings of compassion may be misplaced. It may actually be kinder and more humane to schedule these discussions for the time of day when you're the most alert. You'll then be better prepared to present this bad news in a manner that best suits the situation, demonstrates respect for the employee, and avoids misspeaking in a way that could lead to a grievance or lawsuit.

As you review this inventory, you may also make other important discoveries. You may find that you don't need to be at an energy peak when gathering data and information for your research, although you do need to have a good deal of stamina to write up your results. You may realize that you're so experienced addressing performance problems with students that "you could do it in your sleep," but the same is not true when a faculty member is causing problems for his or her colleagues.

The goal of this exercise, therefore, is to match as many of your A activities (those requiring your highest levels of energy) to the peaks of your energy cycle, your C and D activities (those requiring little or no energy on your part) to the valleys of your energy cycle, and your B activities (those requiring a moderate amount of energy) to times of day when your energy level may be declining but has not yet bottomed out.

The benefit of rescheduling your activities in this way is twofold: You'll get more done because you won't be attempting to engage in activities that require high energy during your low-energy times of day, and your results will be of better quality because you'll be performing those tasks that require your attentiveness during those periods when you're more likely to be alert.

There's also another type of inventory that you can conduct as a way of using your own personal energy cycle to its best advantage. This second inventory, as shown in Table 5.2, doesn't explore when your energy is at its highest but rather where you tend to *expend* that energy. There are four sections of the inventory, each consisting of five statements, which address the following stakeholders in your life and career.

- Yourself
- Your personal inner circle (your family and friends)
- Your professional inner circle (your stakeholders and supervisors)
- Your outer circle (society as a whole)

Read each statement and then check the appropriate box indicating how often you engage in the activity described. Since no two weeks are ever alike, try to think in terms of what usually happens as opposed to what is happening this week in particular or what happens during particularly good or bad weeks.

You score this inventory by assigning yourself five points each time you checked a box in the "Five or More Days a Week" column, three points each time you checked a box in the "Two to Four Days a Week" column, and no points each time you checked a box in the "One Day a Week or Never" column. Your final score, if you've calculated it correctly, should range between 0 and 100. You can interpret it as follows:

- If you scored from 70 to 100 points, you appear to be using your energy wisely. You're taking care of yourself, being attentive to the people you

Table 5.2 Personal Energy Use Inventory

5 or More Days a Week	2 to 4 Days a Week	One Day a Week or Never	Activity
Yourself			
			I get six or more hours of sleep at night.
			I have an hour or more to relax, not think about work, and engage in a personally meaningful activity.
			I am physically active for at least an hour.
			I feel optimistic and look forward to the future.

(Continued)

Table 5.2 Continued

			I do something that gets me out of my comfort zone.
Your Inner Circle (Your Friends and Family)			
			I spend at least an hour of "quality time" with those dearest to me.
			I show appreciation to someone who is dear to me or tell that person how much he or she means to me.
			I listen to someone who is dear to me tell me about how his or her day went and am truly interested in what that person has to say.
			I make a genuine effort to view an issue from the perspective of someone who is dear to me when that perspective differs from my own.
			I initiate contact with someone who is dear to me. (In other words, rather than answering an e-mail or receiving a call, I write a new e-mail message or make a call.)
Your Professional Inner Circle (Your Stakeholders and Supervisors)			
			I have a constructive and serious talk with my supervisor(s) and/or stakeholders about significant, "big picture" issues as opposed to the details of the immediate task at hand.
			I feel appropriately challenged (but not overwhelmed) at work.
			I show appreciation to my supervisor(s) or stakeholders.
			I perform an action or engage in an activity that I find particularly satisfying or meaningful at work.
			I assist someone with a significant task at work even though it's not in my job description and I wasn't instructed by a supervisor to do so.
Your Outer Circle (Society as a Whole)			
			I perform an action or engage in an activity that I can say in all sincerity makes the world a better place.
			I allow someone else to go first (such as when forming a queue or entering a line of traffic) even when it's my turn.

			I give someone else a chance to shine, even if that person is a total stranger, without needing to be the center of attention myself.
			I tip generously and/or sincerely thank someone for his or her service.
			I double check to make sure I'm not inconveniencing anyone else by leaving trash behind or otherwise expecting other people to do something I should have done myself.

care about, treating your colleagues at work well, and making the world a better place. What this score means is that you're not merely an efficient time manager but also that you're directing your energy toward activities that you'll regard as a good investment of time long after they're over.

- If you scored from 30 to 69 points, you're probably like most of the people you meet every day. You know what you should do so as to expend your energy wisely; you're just not engaging in those activities often enough to produce the greatest benefit for the energy expended. Fortunately, the inventory itself can tell you how you can improve. Look at the items for which you had the lowest scores. Choose two of those activities and make a conscious effort to engage in them just one more time per week. Doing so may seem a bit artificial at first, but if you continue to engage in this practice, after a few weeks, you'll find yourself feeling, not merely more productive, but *satisfied* by the way you've redirected your energy toward the things that matter.
- If you scored fewer than 30 points, you may be aware of *when* your energy is the highest, but you don't seem to be using it to your best advantage. You're probably approaching your work (and maybe life itself) as a list of random activities that you're supposed to check off as you do them. That type of behavior may feel efficient and productive but can leave you feeling as though you misspent the energy you had on activities that didn't improve your life or the lives of those around you later. You may feel that you simply don't have enough time in your schedule to engage in the activities listed in this inventory. But you actually do. See if you can use the time and stress management principles discussed in this book to carve out opportunities to perform one or two of the items listed in the inventory *beyond what you're already doing*. In other words, if you're physically active three times a week now, make it your goal to exercise four times a week. If you've never had a habit of tipping generously, start by doing so just once a week. Effective use of energy isn't about making huge changes overnight; it's about small adjustments that add up to something significant over time.

Some readers may be wondering what this inventory has to do with proper time management. "What difference does it make," we can imagine someone saying, "to my productivity and efficiency if I express appreciation to someone dear to me or do something that makes the world a better place?"

The answer is that good time management isn't just about the quantity of what we produce; it's also about the quality of what we do. And if we direct our energy day after day to activities that strike us as meaningless or that make us feel as though our job is nothing more than a way to earn a paycheck, eventually both the quantity *and* the quality of what we produce will decline.

In fact, if you scored on the low end of this inventory, your productivity may already be lower than you assume it is; you're not feeling fulfilled in terms of how you spend your energy, which can lead to disengagement, apathy, inefficiency, and even stress. And that's not good time management or stress management by anyone's standards.

Good use of your energy means that you're not just aware of when you are most alert and have the stamina to engage in important work; it means that you've spent that energy in ways that leave you feeling well-rounded as a person and like a good team member or an employee. After all, finding ways to have more time in your schedule won't be very satisfying if the end result is simply to feel more stressed or exhausted and disengaged from others.

Tracking your energy patterns and how you use that energy complements the earlier techniques we've explored by redirecting your priorities toward activities that will ultimately be most important to you as a person and academic leader. It makes you more efficient *and* more effective, and that results in significantly improved time and stress management.

Chapter 6

Time-Efficient Time Logs and How to Use Them

Another way of gaining a better sense of how you're currently using your time (and thus how you might make needed adjustments to those practices) is to keep a time log. In fact, I've rarely read a book on time management or attended a workshop on this subject that didn't devote considerable attention to the matter of time logs.

As it is usually described, a *time log* is basically a journal in which you record every ten or fifteen minutes throughout the day what you are doing at that moment. For example, you might set your watch or computer to alert you at ten-minute intervals, and, each time the alarm goes off, you jot down a quick note of the time and what you are doing.

It's generally recommended that you record this information for about two weeks since no day is exactly like any other. Then, once you have about ten working days of records, you examine the time log to explore how you're spending your time, whether there are any activities you can eliminate or perform more efficiently, and how you might restructure your day so as to accomplish more of your high-priority goals.

By logging your activities and the time taken to complete them, a time log provides you with useful information that you can use to identify:

- how accurately you estimated the time you'd need for various tasks
- which activities occupy a great deal of time without producing useful results
- when you're most likely to be interrupted during the day
- whether you're effectively matching each task to your energy level during the day
- how crises affect your ability to perform the other responsibilities of your job

There's just one problem with time logs: *No one ever sticks with them.* And why should they? They're huge time wasters. They interrupt your work every ten or fifteen minutes, take you away from your work to write a note, distract you, and probably require you to reconstruct your entire thought process when you return to what you're doing. These are simply not time-efficient activities.

True, they may *lead to* more time-efficient activities, but if you're attracted by the idea of a time log in the first place, you probably feel that you already have too much to do; you don't need one more obligation that consumes precious minutes throughout your day. So, what you can learn from time logs is valuable, but they have to be designed so that the time they save you isn't outweighed (even in the short term) by the time they cost you.

Fortunately, there are two highly time-effective ways to keep a time log. The first is simply to create a table in a word processing document or spreadsheet. Across the top of the table, label each column with the various activities you engage in as an academic leader: respond to e-mail, write memos or e-mails, attend meetings, meet one-on-one with people, teach courses, collect research data, and so on. The particular activities that you engage in are probably not the same as those of other academic leaders, so make your headings as comprehensive as you need to. Next, use a column at the right to break the day into ten- or fifteen-minute blocks.

The result will be something like table 6.1. (Please note that this example is simplified so as to provide a short illustration. Your actual time log will probably have many more columns and will certainly have more rows so as to cover the entire workday.)

Table 6.1 A Time-Efficient Time Log

	Responding to E-mail	Writing Memos or Initiating E-mail	Group Meetings	One-on-One Appointments	Teaching Courses	Preparing for Courses	Collecting Research Data	Interpreting Research Data	Research-related Writing	Meeting with Prospective Donors	Meeting with Prospective Students	Commuting to/from Campus	Conducting Personal Business	Phone Calls
8:00 a.m.														
8:15 a.m.														
8:30 a.m.														
8:45 a.m.														
9:00 a.m.														
9:15 a.m.														

9:30 a.m.										
9:45 a.m.										
10:00 a.m.										
10:15 a.m.										
10:30 a.m.										
10:45 a.m.										
11:00 a.m.										
11:15 a.m.										
11:30 a.m.										
11:45 a.m.										
12:00 p.m.										
12:15 p.m.										
12:30 p.m.										

Then, as in a conventional time log, you set your watch or computer to alert you at each interval indicated in the leftmost column. When the alarm goes off, you simply place a checkmark in the appropriate row for that time in whichever column best indicates what you were doing when you received the alert.

It requires virtually no time at all to record this checkmark on the table, and your work is barely interrupted. Best of all, at the end of the day (or however long you keep this time log), you don't have to sort through your notes to uncover how you were spending large blocks of time: The arrangement of checkmarks will make your time pattern very clear to you.

Suppose, for example, you found that all your checkmarks from 8:00 a.m. until 10:30 a.m. fell in the column headed "Responding to E-mail." That pattern may cause you to wonder whether answering e-mail first thing in the morning is the most efficient use of your time. And if that period happens to overlap with one of your high-energy periods, you may wonder whether it would be better to engage in activities that require more mental focus (such as preparing for class, interpreting research data, or engaging in research-related writing) during this time.

A second alternative to traditional time logs is the use of a smartphone app to track your time. Regardless of the type of smartphone or tablet you use, you simply need to conduct a search for the key words *time log* on whichever app store you regularly visit to download your apps.

Some apps will function similarly to the improved time log we explored earlier: You enter the various types of activities you perform throughout the day, set an interval for your alerts, and then tap the appropriate activity to describe what you're doing whenever you receive an alert. The apps then provide a pie chart that indicates how you spent your time during any given day or week; they can also plot your activities across the day so that you can see how you spent your time in, for example, the early morning versus the late afternoon.

Other time log apps allow you to import information directly from your calendar, allow you to enter start times and stop times for different activities, remind you when it might be useful to move on from one type of activity to another, or allow you to merge mileage and expenses directly into your record of how you spent your time. Since there are so many options, be sure to explore the various possibilities in order to select one that best suits your needs and provides you with all the insights you hope to gain from a time tracker.

Regardless of which form of time log you use, after you've collected as much information as you think appropriate, the next task becomes figuring out what conclusions to draw from the data you've gathered. A good approach to take is to focus on activities that either occupy a great deal of your time (i.e., there are a lot of checkmarks in that column even if they're spaced out) or tend to occur in blocks (i.e., they occupy an hour or more of your time at once even if they don't recur very often). Both of these types of activities may provide an opportunity for *clustering* and organization of tasks into periods of *quality time*.

The idea behind clustering is that we tend to be far more productive and efficient at an activity when we can devote our attention to it without interruption. Although we may think we're being productive when we're multitasking, that's actually an illusion.

Psychologists call the sort of focus we have when we multitask *continuous partial attention*, and the work we do while in that state takes longer than if we performed one activity at a time and is generally of lower quality since we didn't give it our full attention. It's actually the opposite of multitasking—no matter whether we call it unitasking, monotasking, or mindfulness—that gives us our best results.

So, it makes sense to cluster activities that we generally perform sporadically as interruptions to our work (things like answering e-mail or talking on the phone) into single blocks of time and to focus exclusively on other tasks (such as planning and assessment) exclusively during other blocks of time.

Regardless of whether these extended periods of focused activity result from a conscious effort to cluster activities or tend to arise automatically, as indicated by a series of checkmarks grouped together in a column in a time log, it's good time management to schedule those activities for the right time in our energy cycles. If you're a "battery" or "skier" in terms of your energy rhythm (see the previous chapter), it's best to conduct activities that don't require your most focused attention during the "downward energy slope" of your day. If you're a "Bactrian camel" or "trampoline," it may be best to conduct them while you're in an "energy valley" between two peaks. If you're a "plateau," you may want to wait until your extended period of high energy begins to subside. In that way, you will have saved activities that require more energy for times when you *have* more energy and not squandered your best hours for productivity on straightening up your desk or sitting in a dull meeting that you could easily have scheduled for another time.

Quality time occurs when we take this concept further and plan regular clusters of our activities into our schedules so that we have the opportunities we need for proper focus and attention. Each academic leader's specific use of quality time will vary according to his or her own specific needs and position, but the following are a few examples of blocks you may wish to include in your schedule.

- A *clinic* is a block of time you set aside for people for "drop-ins" when appointments aren't necessary. This prevents people from having to make an appointment to see you in order to ask a quick question or have a routine document signed. Clinics are useful because stakeholders know when you'll be able to be reached for simple matters. They won't run the risk of coming to your office repeatedly only to find you in a meeting or appointment. Clinics help make an "open door policy" actually possible for time-strapped, busy administrators.
- *Rounds* are regularly scheduled trips outside the office to tour the facilities in your area, have impromptu conversations with whomever you meet, and address issues informally. Academic leaders sometimes believe that going on rounds is a luxury they just can't afford in their already crowded schedules, but they're actually excellent "investments" of time. While you're on rounds, you might encounter someone with a minor issue that you can address long before it grows into a major crisis. You can learn about some of the good things people are doing, not just the bad things that get brought to your office as complaints. And you can have conversations with stakeholders in their own areas, leaving when you need to, not when they decide to (which often is the case when they're in your office).
- A *quiet hour* is a period when everyone in your office focuses exclusively on paperwork. Appointments and meetings are not allowed. Calls are directed immediately to voice mail. E-mail is turned off. In offices where we've done this, people have always been surprised at how productive they become. The truth is that a report that might have taken you several days to write when you were repeatedly interrupted by phone calls and drop-in visitors can often be completed in under an hour when you're able to devote your full attention to it.
- *E-mail time* is a set period when you catch up on reading and responding to e-mails. If you establish a fixed block of e-mail time every day, it still

allows you to get back to someone within twenty-four hours. (That may take a little bit of adjustment in environments where people are used to instant answers, but people do adjust.) But it also means that you're not distracted from other important projects by the frequent arrival of new e-mail messages.

- *Phone time* is the same as e-mail time, except that it is the period during which you'll make and receive phone calls. There is the possibility, of course, that if you have a specific schedule for phone time, and so does the person you're trying to reach by telephone, you could never reach one another but instead end up playing "phone tag." That is certainly possible, but there's an easy solution (as there is to any occurrence of phone tag): Simply use the phone messages you leave and receive as a means of establishing a mutually agreed on time for a phone appointment, and conduct the call then even if it is outside of your regular phone time.
- Perhaps the most important form of quality time is what I call *Appointments with Yourself.* These are scheduled tasks that include such activities as conducting research, writing reports, drafting letters of recommendation, and the like. Appointments with yourself are when you'll handle most of the truly important activities you have to do—the rocks in your division of rocks, pebbles, and sand—by blocking out time so that it doesn't get eaten up by trivial administrative tasks.

One of the great advantages of quality time is that it imposes a structure on work, allowing you to move away from reactive work to proactive work. In other words, rather than just responding to requests and problems as they arise, you use quality time to get done higher-priority tasks that can handle requests even before they're made and prevent problems from occurring in the first place.

Chapter 7

The Care and Feeding of To-Do Lists

To-do lists are similar to time logs in that, if done well, they can be terrific tools for effective time management but, if done poorly, they simply waste time that academic leaders don't have to spare. A well-constructed to-do list can:

- help you prioritize the things you have to accomplish
- help you work much more efficiently
- motivate you to get more done

On the other hand, if you don't create the right kind of to-do list, it can:

- *de*motivate you by causing you to see unfinished projects that remain on your list day after day
- waste a lot of time as you try to reorganize and re-sort the list
- multiply into competing lists, such as things to do at the office, things to do at home, things to do in the long term, things to do immediately, and so on

The unfortunate truth is that most academic leaders have the later kind of list, and so, rather than helping them become more efficient, the lists just become one more obstacle to effective time management.

When we don't care for our to-do lists properly, they become the masters of us, not us of them. They nag us day after day with their catalogs of unaccomplished projects, making us feel like failures because we never get anything done. And so, just to gain some sense of accomplishment, we write something on the list that we were going to do anyway (or worse, just completed) for the sheer pleasure of crossing it off. That's not an effective use of our time.

But to-do lists can be extremely helpful if we simply keep in mind several key principles.

TO-DO LISTS ARE FOR TASKS, NOT PROJECTS

Effective time managers never put any item on their to-do lists that they can't complete in a single session. Or, to put it another way, they never put any item on their lists that would take more than an hour to complete. Table 7.1 shows a few examples that may clarify this piece of advice.

There are several things wrong with the to-do list items in the left column. To begin with, it would be very difficult to tell whether you actually completed some of them in a meaningful way. What does it mean to go to the library? Is just stopping off there to return a book what you had in mind, or were you thinking of devoting a full day to intense background research? It's far better to identify one or more specific tasks that you intend to accomplish at the library and put those tasks on your list. In that way, you'll know exactly what you hope to accomplish and be able to tell when you've actually done what you set out to do.

The other thing that's wrong with many of the items in the left column is that they're actually projects, not tasks. Unless it's a very short, easy article, you're not going to be able to write a complete article in just one sitting. And what do you mean by "Write article" anyway? Do you mean create the first draft? Complete a polished version that you can submit to a journal? Something in between? Without that type of clarification, items are going to remain on your to-do list for a very long time, making you feel as though you're accomplishing very little and not doing anything at all to improve your time or stress management.

Table 7.1 Projects versus Tasks

On a To-Do List, Don't Put This	Instead Put This
Go to the library	Spend half an hour in the library reading current articles on tensions within the European Union
Write article	Find five sources for a literature review and prepare annotated bibliography entries for them
Revise syllabus	Select the primary textbook to be listed in the revised syllabus
Conduct assessment project	Write three learning outcomes that can be included in the assessment project

There's a clear benefit in using a to-do list to record tasks, not projects: Doing so forces you to break complex projects down into meaningful steps. You can think of what you're doing as a simple form of *project management*, deciding what needs to be done in what order so as to accomplish an ambitious goal.

Writing down items like "Revise syllabus" and "Conduct assessment project" doesn't tell you where to begin. But if you force yourself to break these complex projects down into a series of tasks you can do in one sitting, you'll know exactly where you have to begin. And you'll be much more likely to make progress quickly because identifying a good textbook or drafting three learning outcomes doesn't seem as overwhelming as completing an entire project would. They're merely tasks that you can perform in an hour or less and then check them off your to-do list with a great feeling of accomplishment.

DON'T JUST LIST TASKS; SCHEDULE THEM

The best place to keep your to-do list isn't on a blank piece of paper; it's on your calendar. You're much more likely to take positive action and actually accomplish something if you make it one of those appointments with yourself that we explored in chapter 6. Alone as a bullet point on a piece of paper, "Select the primary textbook to be listed in the revised syllabus" may not seem all that compelling. But if it shows up on your calendar as what you're supposed to do at 9:30 a.m. on Tuesday, you'll probably get it done by 10:30, maybe even by 10:00.

Remember the temptation we noted earlier to do what's urgent rather than what's important because most people take deadlines seriously? Here's an instance where you can tap into your natural tendency to want to complete what's urgent and channel that urge toward better time management. In essence, what you've done is taken a task that may have been important but not urgent and made it seem both urgent and important by scheduling it on your calendar. So, rather than prioritizing your schedule, what you're doing is *scheduling your priorities*.

USE APPS OR STICKY NOTES FOR BETTER SCHEDULING

Just as apps for your smartphone or tablet made keeping a time log much easier than trying to write down on paper everything you do throughout the day, so can an app help you organize your to-do list. If you search the key words *to-do list* wherever you acquire your apps, you're likely to get several dozen possibilities to choose from.

Many allow you to keep your to-do list items organized in multiple formats. For example, you can see all the items on your list in an order of priority (the usual way we order the items on to-do lists), but the app will also search for open spots on your schedule and suggest assigning the task to that time. You can always refuse the suggestion and move the task to a different spot on your calendar, but merely having to make that decision causes you to think about the best time for the activity and make a commitment to yourself that you'll complete the activity then.

If you'd prefer a less technological solution, another good alternative to the traditional to-do list on paper is to write each task on a separate sticky note. This variation has a number of advantages over a simple list of tasks.

First, since sticky notes come in different colors, you can code your activities in ways that are meaningful to you: teaching tasks, research tasks, administrative tasks, household errands, and so on. Second, since sticky notes can be reorganized easily, you can change the order of the tasks on your list as your priorities change. Third, since sticky notes can be attached to almost anything, you can post them on a paper calendar to make an appointment with yourself, or put them somewhere where they are difficult to overlook (such as attached to your computer monitor, the door to your office, or the steering wheel of your car). The flexibility of these notes increases the likelihood that you'll see the task and complete it in a timely manner.

USE A SYSTEM THAT IDENTIFIES YOUR HIGHEST PRIORITIES

If your to-do list contains only two or three items, it's probably not very difficult to determine which of those tasks is most important. But most academic leaders have to-do lists with ten, twenty, or more different tasks they need to accomplish. And it's very difficult to figure out where to begin when your to-do list is very long. That's why you need a system that lets you quickly identify your highest priorities. Since different people will be attracted to different systems, I'll give you three choices, and you can select the one you think will work best for you.

The Paired Comparisons System

The Paired Comparisons System begins with a principle we just encountered: When you have only two items on your to-do list, it's easy to tell which is the most important. So, with this system, you look at only two items at a time.

Take the first two tasks or goals on your to-do list, and ask yourself: Which of these is more important? If it's the first of the two items, you retain that one and set the second item aside. Then you go onto the third item on the list. Now which is more important: the first item or the third? If it's the third item, you keep that one and set the first aside. Take the fourth item on the list: Is it more important than the third? In this way, you go through your entire list, and, by the end, you'll have the item, task, or goal that is most important to you.

After experimenting with the Paired Comparisons System a few times, you'll find that you can perform this type of sorting relatively quickly. It's thus a good way to start the workday or to make sure that you're devoting any "recovered time" (such as an open block on your schedule that suddenly appears because a meeting gets canceled) to the tasks that really matter. In fact, after a few attempts, you may find that you don't even need to sort through the entire list. A brief scan in which you ask yourself, "Is this the most important objective I have right now?" will quickly allow you to focus on your highest priorities.

The Deadline/Payoff System

With the Deadline/Payoff System, you assign each item on your list two values: a deadline value and a payoff value. The deadline value involves how soon that item may need to be completed. If it's in the distant future, perhaps more than six months from now, assign that item a 1. If it's due a few weeks or months from now, assign it a 2. If it's due in the next few days, assign it a 3. Then give each item a payoff value. If it's not likely to have much impact or visibility, give it a 2. If it'll have a moderate amount of impact or visibility, give it a 4. And if it's going to be seen by or affect a lot of people, give it a 6.

Then add the numbers together for each item and sort your list from the highest score to the lowest. What you're really doing in this system is taking both urgency (the deadline value) and importance (the impact value) into account. But the system favors importance over urgency by assigning impact scores that are twice the value of the deadline scores. In this way, a very important task with a long deadline will receive a higher score (7) than an insignificant item with an immediate deadline (5).

The system thus helps you avoid squandering your time on those activities that won't matter very much once you complete them and guides you toward investing your time where it'll make the greatest difference.

The One-at-a-Time System

The One-at-a-Time System tends to be favored by people who prefer just to dive right in to their tasks and not be distracted by having to sort through their lists or assign and calculate scores. There are three major variations of the One-at-a-Time System:

- *Do the hardest task first*. This approach is based on the way many seven-year-olds eat their dinner. When forced to eat everything on their plates, many children will gobble up whatever food they like least before they eat anything else. By doing so, they get it out of the way, and they then can enjoy the foods they prefer. In time management, you use this approach by taking on first whichever task you personally find the hardest or are dreading the most. In that way, everything else on your to-do list seems easier, and you're much more likely to keep going and complete more of the activities that remain on the list.
- *Do the easiest task first*. Some people prefer to reverse the previous method and tackle the easiest task on their to-do list first. By doing so, they feel a sense of accomplishment—"Here we are, only ten minutes into the workday, and I've already checked one item off my to-do list."—and are then inspired to go on to more demanding tasks. The one caution you need to observe in adopting this approach, however, is to do only one easy task "to prime the pump." If you keep only doing the easiest items on your list, you may never get to the hardest items, even if they're far more important than the easy items, because you keep putting them off.
- *The Ivy Lee/Charles Schwab Method*: Ivy Lee (1877–1934) was an efficiency expert who explained to the head of U.S. Steel Charles M. Schwab (1862–1939) his system for improving the time management skills of corporate executives. Each day before going home, Schwab was instructed to create a list of the six most important things he had to do the next day in order of priority. Then, when he arrived at work, he was to start doing the items on his list and not do anything else until all six tasks were complete. If Schwab never got to anything else, that was fine: He was still devoting his time to the six most important things he had to do. If he never got beyond the first one or two items on his list, that was still fine: Even then, he was working on the most important things he had to do. Schwab tried this system and discovered that it greatly improved his efficiency and time management skills.

The goal of each piece of advice we've considered in this chapter is the same: Transform a randomly ordered to-do list into a prioritized schedule of tasks. In this way, you'll be much more likely to accomplish the things you need to do and less likely to find yourself burdened with a long list of projects that never seem to get done.

Chapter 8

Handling Documents Efficiently

Paperwork can be the bane of the academic leader's existence. Administrators are expected to generate a large number of reports, proposals, e-mails, forms, and memos, plus there's another huge mound of documents in the sheer amount of material they're expected to read, digest, and file. The documents involved in academic administration are both electronic and printed, and they may range from the vitally important to the hopelessly trivial.

Getting a handle on how to deal with these documents efficiently can be a real key to good time management. It can keep us from wasting precious moments sorting for an important document that we need and devoting a major part of our workdays to reading and responding to items that are insignificant.

Why do we allow our offices to become cluttered, thus making it more difficult for us to be productive and find what we need easily? There may be several reasons:

- *Bottlenecks*. Academic leaders have a wide range of stakeholders. They may receive documents from students, faculty members, staff members, parents, other administrators, donors and potential donors, members of the community, and other constituencies. In many cases, those documents require a response and, in the course of an overscheduled workday, just finding the time to keep up with the mail and e-mail can be difficult.
- *The "I Might Need This Someday" Fallacy*. Although our institutions have policies about how long certain types of documents must be retained, we tend to keep others because we think they might be useful at some point. We forget that there's almost always another copy of the same document available to us elsewhere, and so we end up saving far more than we need.
- *The "Creative Minds Have Cluttered Desks" Fallacy*. Many people have the assumption that innovative people are too busy doing "important" things

to keep their desks and offices tidy. But there's absolutely no correlation at all between neatness (or the lack thereof) and creativity. You can be just as creative—and probably more so—in a well-organized environment as you can when you're surrounded by stacks of paper.
- *The "Having It On My Desk Saves Me Time" Fallacy.* Some people assume that they're being more efficient by "saving" time from filing and organizing through all the stacks of disorganized paper around them. That's actually a misconception. A well-organized and consistent filing system will actually save you much more time in the long run because you'll always know exactly where everything is.

The best way to avoid these problems is to adopt a time-efficient system for dealing with documents known as the *OHIO Method*. In this acronym, the word OHIO has nothing to do with the midwestern state or the Japanese word for "good morning." It stands for the phrase *Only Handle It Once*. The idea is that every time you encounter a document, no matter whether it's electronic or on paper, you make an immediate decision about what to do with it and deal with that document right then and there.

The OHIO Method involves making one of the following four choices about each document you receive:

1. *Do It*. If the document requires a response that you can provide immediately, you're much more efficient in terms of time management if you take care of it at once than if you procrastinate. Frequently, we put off dealing with the document because it requires us to do something unpleasant such as turn down a request or address someone's inappropriate behavior. But you'll have to engage in that unpleasant activity anyway, so it's better to get it out of the way now than to delay the inevitable. In fact, doing the disagreeable task immediately can actually make you feel less frustrated by your job. Instead of being burdened for hours or days with the idea that you still have this difficult response to make, you get it behind you, thus allowing yourself to move on to parts of your job that you may enjoy more.
2. *Delegate It*. Remember what we said in chapter 4 about time being only one of the resources that academic leaders have available to them? You can also take advantage of *people* resources to accomplish some of the tasks that come your way. In many cases, a document may end up in your office that simply isn't worth your time to address. Maybe it's a request for a report of information that is available to others in your area. Maybe a simple reply or form letter is all that's required. Maybe completing this task will help someone else develop his or her own leadership skills. If any of these possibilities exist, the time-efficient response is to assign the

document to someone else to deal with, make your expectations known as to how you want the matter addressed, and then move on to other activities that require your individual expertise.

3. *Defer It.* Some of the documents that reach you by e-mail or land on your desk will require more prolonged action than you can give them immediately. These are the documents that you'll defer acting on. But you shouldn't simply put them off by saying "I'll get back to these items sometime." That's how things pile up in our offices and why we start falling behind in our work. Instead, make your best estimate as to how long it will take to deal with that document and then schedule one of those Appointments with Yourself that we talked about in chapter 6. Block out the time you'll need to deal with the document, put a reminder on your calendar, and make a commitment that when that "appointment" occurs, you'll address the document in such a way that you can clear it out of your inbox once and for all.

4. *Discard It.* Another category of items that we receive by regular mail or e-mail contains documents that we don't need to act upon at all or even keep. It consists of advertisements for products and services that we would never use, catalogs of merchandise that are also available online, and other unsolicited material that's of no immediate value. Discarding this material immediately keeps your office neater (thus improving the efficiency of your workspace in your nexus of resources; see chapter 4) at the same time that it avoids time-wasting activities like having to sort catalogs and unnecessary papers when searching for a more important document, being distracted from your work by attractive images of products that don't help you accomplish your goals, and repeatedly needing to reorganize your desk and office shelves. Much of the worthless e-mail that comes our way is sent to us via listservs. All listservs are required to provide an easy method by which you can unsubscribe from them either by clicking on a link or by replying to them with the word *UNSUBSCRIBE* at the start of your text. The few seconds it takes to remove yourself from these lists can save you precious time later as you receive additional e-mails advertising goods, services, and events that are of no interest to you.

The OHIO Method is a great way to deal with documents efficiently and to prevent your e-mail inbox from being filled with messages and your office from overflowing with paper. But what do you do if you already have thousands of messages in your e-mail inbox and stacks of paper all over your office? Let's address the e-mail problem first.

Because of the number of constituencies they serve, academic leaders receive a large number of e-mail messages. If you follow the OHIO Method—writing a quick but cordial reply to messages during daily E-mail

Time (see chapter 6) and then deleting them unless they require further action—you'll find yourself annoying people less because they're not waiting for hours or days for a response, and fewer messages will simply "slip through the cracks" because you forget about them before having a chance to reply. As for all of the existing messages in your inbox, you can deal with them by doing the following:

1. Take *all* the messages that arrived prior to this moment and shift them from your inbox to an e-mail archive. By archiving them, you're not deleting them; they'll still be available to you if you need them, but they won't be cluttering your inbox and interfering with your time efficiency. If you're like most academic leaders, you'll discover that you'll never need to consult that e-mail archive at all and, after a few months, you'll feel safe simply deleting it.
2. There is a chance, even though it is small, that by moving these messages to an archive, you may be overlooking some message that required a reply but that you haven't yet been able to address. Almost certainly when this happens, the person will send you a follow-up reminder by e-mail. When that occurs, reply to that person during your next available E-mail Time, apologizing for your late response by saying that you're shifting to a new system of handling your e-mail and that this message inadvertently got caught up in the transition. Address the person's issue in full, and then delete the message.
3. Continue keeping your e-mail inbox purged by rigorously applying the OHIO Method to all incoming messages from this point forward. When you leave the office at the end of the day, your e-mail inbox should be completely empty.
4. When you are away from the office and unable to respond to new messages that day, post an away message that informs everyone writing you that you are out of the office and when you are likely to be able to respond. If you have a trusted assistant who can handle routine matters for you, consider having your messages forwarded to this person for the duration of your time away and empower this person to act on all appropriate items so as to reduce the number of replies you'll need to send when you return.

Dealing with the actual paper documents that fill your office requires a somewhat similar approach. But this time, we can break the process into three simple steps:

1. *Sorting.* If the prospect of cleaning your entire workspace all at once seems overwhelming, start with small bits of time. Set a timer and sort

through materials for half an hour, even fifteen minutes if half an hour is too big a block for your schedule. Then, as you sort, follow this powerful but rarely discussed principle: *Examine each document while standing up.* When we sit down while going through our papers, we're more likely to be distracted. Some document or other will catch our attention and then, rather than dealing with it, we start reading it and reminiscing. But when we stand up, while sorting through our papers, our approach becomes more business-like. The task takes on some urgency, and we get much more done within the same amount of time.
2. *Purging.* As you sort, apply the OHIO Method. Touch each item only once and make a quick decision about what you'll do with it. Discard any document that you could get a copy of elsewhere or that is no longer useful. If a document requires a more thoughtful response, don't become distracted by it: Schedule a task on your calendar that allows as much time as you'll need to deal with that document, and address it then. As you come to items that must be filed, sort them into groups: invoices, budget reports, personnel materials, and so on. Ask yourself, "Do my institution's policies require me to keep this? If not, do I really need or want it?" Your general principle should be: *When in doubt, throw it out.*
3. *Maintaining a Routine.* Once you've started organizing your documents in this way, keep it up. Block out a regular time on your calendar for filing and dealing with clutter. Choose an amount of time that seems right to you: fifteen minutes a day, a half hour at the end of each week, whatever suits the rhythms of your work. Also use the "time puddles" that we discussed in chapter 2 for time-efficient purging. For example, in the few minutes you might otherwise spend waiting for someone to return a phone call, you could deal with five to ten documents and get them off your desk. For items that you do need to save, use file cabinets, plastic containers, and other accessories for shelves and closets that allow for easy organization and access to the material when you need it.

While this approach works for most people, it's important to note that a strong dissenting voice has argued that people who try to break the task of organizing their environment into multiple, short neatening sessions often lose their commitment after only a few attempts. In the book *The Life-Changing Magic of Tidying Up: The Japanese Art of Decluttering and Organizing*, Marie Kondo argues that neatening should be a *once and done* activity.

A commitment to a tidy workspace should be for life. People who diet often find that their weight increases again after they reach their targets, while people who change their eating habits and lifestyle permanently are more likely to maintain a healthy weight. In much the same way, Kondo suggests that the commitment to a neat office (or house) should involve an entire restructuring of what we keep, what we discard, and how we return items to their proper place after we've used them.

Which approach is likely to work best for you: neatening up in multiple, short sessions or a massive purging of your workspace followed by a commitment to a new, neater way of working? To help you decide, take a look at table 8.1 and ask yourself which approach worked best for you in the past when trying to achieve the goal listed in the leftmost column: Did you get better results when you tried to do things little-by-little or all at once? Please keep in mind that this inventory is not about which approach you *liked best* or *found more enjoyable* but about *which was more effective*.

You'll probably find that you have checkmarks in both columns, but does one column have a clear majority of your marks? If you've usually had your best results doing things gradually, then your neatening up is also likely to be more successful if you do it in small batches. If you were more effective completing projects from start to finish all at once, then Marie Kondo's system will probably be your best option.

CREATING ELECTRONIC DOCUMENTS FROM PAPER

Another effective way of gaining control of all the documents that come to us as academic leaders is to convert them from paper to electronic forms.

Table 8.1 Gradual versus All-at-Once Systems

Goal	Little by Little?	All at Once?
Losing weight		
Getting toned		
Overcoming a habit (e.g., smoking)		
Writing an article/paper		
Completing a syllabus/project		
Packing for or unpacking from a move		
Buying/wrapping holiday gifts		
Researching and buying a car		
Finding a new house/apartment		
Submitting job applications		
Breaking off a bad relationship		
Running multiple errands		

Many photocopiers also serve as scanners. But dedicated document scanners sometimes have advantages that printers and photocopiers lack.

- Some printers and photocopiers simply transform the document into an *image*, while dedicated document scanners are often able to transform a paper document into *machine readable text* such as a word processing document or spreadsheet. The advantage of machine readable text is that it's searchable if you're looking for a particular word or phrase. It also enables you to cut and paste text from one electronic document to another.
- Some dedicated document scanners can recognize the type of document they are processing and handle the information it contains in a specialized manner. For example, when scanning a business card, they can add the information to your address book. When scanning a receipt, they can add the information to a spreadsheet. And when scanning a memo or letter, they can create a file in Adobe's PDF (Portable Document Format). Often, these dedicated scanners do so by having slots of different sizes for business cards, receipts, and other papers to be fed into.

In short, organizing your workspace can help you better organize your time and vice versa. But remember that being neat and being organized are not the same thing. There are academic leaders whose offices look pristine but who are unsystematic in their other work habits.

Chapter 9

Making SMART Goals Even SMARTER

Sometimes we're not as efficient as we'd like to be because we haven't clarified in our minds exactly what we'd like to accomplish. We may know, for instance, that we'd like to reduce the degree of conflict between those two faculty members who are always arguing at meetings or that we'd like to align our program's goals more closely with those of our institution's strategic plan. But if someone were to ask us precisely how we intended to do those things, we'd probably be at a loss as to how to respond.

That inability to clarify our goals in this way can be what's preventing us from getting anything done. It's very hard to know what to do when you have only a vague idea of what it is you want to accomplish.

In 1981, George Doran, Arthur Miller, and James Cunningham developed a simple acronym that has helped many people focus their goals in a way that increases the likelihood those goals will actually be accomplished. Their idea was to transform goals into SMART Goals, with the letters in SMART standing for Specific, Measurable, Achievable, Responsible, and Time-Related (Doran, Miller, and Cunningham, 1981).

Since this original version of the SMART Goals concept was published, there have been many attempts to refine it. Achievable is sometimes replaced with Attainable, Appropriate, or Ambitious; Responsible is sometimes exchanged for Relevant, Reasonable, or Results-Based; and Time-Related is sometimes rephrased as Timely, Time-Specific, or something similar. Regardless of the precise formulation, the goal of the acronym is to cause us to clarify our goals in ways similar to the questions listed in Table 9.1.

By checking our goals (and even the tasks recorded on our to-do lists) against these five criteria, we make it much more likely that we'll actually

Table 9.1 SMART Goals

S	Specific	• Have you made it as clear as possible what you want to obtain, why you want to obtain it, how you will obtain it, and which requirements you'll have to meet in order to consider the goal achieved? • Have you phrased your goal in such a way that any ambiguous language has been removed? Would anyone who read your phrasing of the goal understand precisely what you want to do?
M	Measurable	• Do you have a clear and unmistakable way of knowing whether your goal has been achieved? • Is your goal quantifiable in some way? In other words, will you know that you're on track if you've increased or decreased doing something by a certain amount or percentage?
A	Achievable	• Do you have the proper knowledge, experience, and resources available to accomplish this goal? • Is the goal worthwhile, relevant to your longer plans, and feasible given the realities of your situation?
R	Responsible	• Is there some specific person (either yourself or a delegate) who will be personally accountable for progress toward this goal? In other words, have you identified a particular "go-to person" who will be everyone's primary contact regarding this goal? • Is the goal responsibly selected? In other words, have you made sure that you're not sacrificing long-term objectives for short-term gains? Does the goal take matters of efficiency, sustainability, and the common good into account?
T	Time-Related	• Have you set a realistic but ambitious deadline for when this goal should be achieved? • Is the deadline firm or flexible? In other words, would significant harm be caused if the deadline were missed?

accomplish what we need to do in a timely manner. For example, here's the way in which goals are commonly phrased in higher education:

> We need to do something to improve the retention rate in our undergraduate Time and Stress Management degree.

Thinking that we'll get anything accomplished in this way fails the SMART Goals test across the board. Do *what*? *Which* retention rate? (First-year to second-year? Lower division to upper division? All the way to graduation?

Something else?) Improve the rate by *how much*? (Would a 0.05 percent increase be sufficient? Would you not regard yourself as successful if you achieved anything less than triple the current retention rate?) *When* does this need to occur? *Who* is going to be responsible for making this happen?

By using the SMART Goals criteria, we can thus take a vaguely conceived *project* and transform it into a set of time-efficient *tasks* that we'll probably actually complete. Our new series of goals may thus look something like the following:

> By April 15, [YEAR] *[TIME-RELATED]*, the Department of Time and Stress Management will complete a review of three similar programs with better six-year graduation rates than its own and identify no fewer than five best practices these programs are engaged in that have resulted in improved rates of student retention from matriculation through graduation. *[SPECIFIC]* The best practices identified must be
>
> - cost-neutral to the department's budget, *[ACHIEVABLE]*
> - able to be implemented no later than December 1, [YEAR] *[TIME-RELATED]*, and
> - regarded as successful if they result in no less than a 10 percent increase in the Department of Time and Stress Management six-year matriculation-to-graduation rate no later than the spring semester graduation of [YEAR]. *[MEASURABLE]*
>
> Dr. Expeditious will be the primary contact person on this project. *[RESPONSIBLE]*

The advantage of phrasing the department's goals in this way is that it allows everyone in the program to know exactly what needs to be done, who will be in charge of making sure it gets done, when the results have to be achieved, and which conditions or restrictions apply to the tasks.

Nevertheless, for all their advantages over the ways in which we usually try to accomplish things in higher education, SMART Goals do have one noticeable inefficiency as identified by Chip and Dan Heath, who are internationally recognized experts on change and process management.

> The specificity of SMART goals is a great cure for the worst sins of goal setting—ambiguity and irrelevance ("We are going to delight our customers every day in every way!"). But SMART goals are better for steady-state situations than for change situations, because the assumptions underlying them are that the goals are worthwhile. . . . SMART goals presume the emotion; they don't generate it. . . . There are some people whose hearts are set aflutter by goals such as "improving the liquidity ratio by 30 percent over the next 18 months." They're called accountants. (Heath and Heath, 2013, 82)

In other words, SMART Goals work fine for the typical tasks we want to accomplish as academic leaders. But they tend to be less effective when we want to promote a significant and lasting change.

That's because the level of specificity they require may impress the mind, but it doesn't engage the heart. And in order to sustain the level of commitment needed to see a large change project through to the end, all parties involved in the process need to have a considerable amount of emotional investment.

That's an insight that's lost on far too many chancellors, presidents, and provosts. They kick off new strategic planning initiatives by announcing such goals as:

- We're going to improve our first-year to second-year retention rate by 12 percent!
- We're going to move from #516 in the *U.S. News & World Reports* annual rankings to the Top 300!
- We're going to be recognized as the fastest improving university in the state!

And then they wonder why the faculty and staff lose interest in these targets after a few months. Much of what we do in college administration is driven by outcomes and performance metrics. So, we as academic leaders need to be aware of their importance and strive to meet them.

But we also need to realize that the stakeholders we need to involve in achieving these goals—the faculty, staff, and students—are frequently left cold by such matters as retention and graduation rates, national rankings, and perceptions of external observers about whether a school is "improved" or "among the best." They care more about their day-to-day experience and the quality of life that is produced by their association with the college or university.

Sure, it's more fun to be part of a "winning team" than a "losing team." But that pride lasts a few days at most. Coursework, research, and daily life then begin to seem far more important.

For this reason, we may want to convert our SMART Goals to even SMARTER Goals by adding two additional factors to the way in which we set our objectives, particularly when we're communicating those objectives to others. (See Table 9.2.)

If SMART Goals help people understand more precisely what needs to be done in order to meet their objectives in a timely manner, SMARTER Goals also help people *care* about meeting those objectives. And, if people don't care, they're likely to become distracted by other priorities before they finally complete their tasks.

Before we conclude this discussion of goals and their relationship to time management, it might be useful to review a few best practices to use when setting goals. While several of these recommendations may not relate directly

Table 9.2 The Requirements for SMARTER Goals

E	Enthusiasm	• Do you sincerely care about this goal? • Does the goal reflect your core values? • Who are the stakeholders who are necessary for this goal to be achieved? What do they tend to become enthusiastic about? • Can you articulate this goal in such a way that it addresses the interests and core values of the people whose buy-in is required to achieve the goal?
R	Rewards	• What are the milestones you'll cross along the way toward this goal? How will you celebrate short-term progress when you reach one of these milestones? • How will you celebrate long-term completion of the goal? • What will stakeholders regard as suitable recompense for the sacrifices they'll make in achieving this goal?

to how you manage your time, they all relate to time management at least *indirectly*. That's because the better we are at articulating our goals in ways that makes them achievable, the better we are at using our time in ways that help us achieve our priorities and avoid wasting time.

Best practices in setting goals suggest that we should always ask ourselves the following questions:

- Have you stated the goal in positive language? That is to say, have you expressed what you *want to happen*, not what you *hope to avoid*?
- Have you set the goal with a positive intention? In other words, is the goal ethical and likely to benefit you and others?
- Have you identified the most likely factors that could prevent you from achieving this goal? Have you established contingency plans to deal with those factors?
- Is the goal as you've envisioned it too big? Would you increase the likelihood that you'll make timely progress if you were to break your one overarching goal down into smaller goals?
- Will you have to give anything up in order to achieve this goal? Will making progress toward the goal have a negative impact on you in some way (or on your family, friends, work, relationships, or lifestyle)?
- What will happen if, for whatever reason, you don't achieve this goal? How would lack of success make you feel? Do you need a fallback plan?

And to these best practices, we might add one other that I call the *Money Ball Principle* since it relates to a central theme in Michael Lewis's book *Moneyball* (2003) and the Brad Pitt film based on it: Most people fail to achieve their goals because they try to do great things. *The secret to achieving* your goals is not in doing great things, but in doing small things consistently great.

Like most of what we learn about managing time and stress, the Money Ball Principle works equally well in our professional lives as academic leaders and in our personal lives as ordinary people. Moreover, when we're dealing with the type of personal goals that we might call *life goals*—the sorts of objectives that don't affect our career for a few weeks or a few months but that can change our lives entirely—another useful perspective can be what is called the *altitude model*.

With the altitude model, you envision your progression toward the goal as though you were flying in an airplane, with your to-do list for today as the airport where you will land. You then break the single life goal into a series of projects (and ultimately tasks) by asking yourself the following questions:

- *30,000 Feet View*: What do you want your legacy to be? How do you want people to remember you?
- *20,000 Feet View*: In order to leave that legacy behind, what will you need to have achieved ten years from now?
- *10,000 Feet View*: In order to be on track to accomplish that within ten years, what will you need to have done five years from now?
- *5,000 Feet View*: In order to be well positioned to achieve that objective five years from now, what will you need to have done three years from now?
- *3,000 Feet View*: If you truly intend to accomplish that within three years, what will you need to have done next year?
- *1,000 Feet View*: To make that plan possible, what will you need to do within the next six months to one year?
- *Landing*: So, what do all of these answers mean you should be doing *today*?

SMART Goals, SMARTER Goals, best practices in setting goals, and the altitude model all have a single aim: to help us see our goals not as vague hopes and dreams but as achievable yet also aspirational tasks that we can start working on immediately in order to accomplish more of our priorities within a timely manner.

Chapter 10

Avoiding Black Holes of Time

Simply because an activity is time-consuming doesn't mean it isn't worthwhile. In fact, many of the things that academic leaders do—drafting grant applications, preparing budget proposals, evaluating members of the faculty and staff, preparing long-term plans, and the like—require days, weeks, or even months.

But there are also activities that are popularly known as *time sucks*: inefficient or unproductive processes that waste time and produce few, if any, lasting results. An alternative way of describing these activities is to refer to them as *black holes of time*, a useful metaphor that helps us envision pursuits that are so time-consuming that they seem to absorb every available minute we have; they pull time into them but produce nothing important to us as a result.

The first important thing to realize about black holes of time is that *they aren't the same for everyone*. To someone who loves playing video games and finds the excitement and adventure they contain to be life-enriching, engaging in this activity is a worthwhile investment of time. To someone who doesn't share that passion, spending hour after hour before a screen striving to move up a level or two in an imaginary world appears to be nothing more than a black hole of time.

But there's also a second important thing to realize about black holes of time: We engage in certain activities simply because that's what we've always done or because other people seem to expect us to find value in these activities even if we don't. One of the most productive steps you can take, therefore, in promoting effective time management is to identify those processes you're engaging in that are substantially more time-consuming than they are productive and to free yourself from activities that are truly inefficient and that may even make your work harder.

One obvious place to look for black holes of time as an academic leader is the meetings you attend. Our days are often filled with meetings that result in very little value even though they consume vast amounts of time. Frequently, we have meetings because that's the schedule that our predecessor established, or we think we ought to get together with people so that we can all stay "in the loop." But if meetings get in the way of our efficiency, they're actually more harmful than they're worth.

As an academic leader, therefore, we can improve our time efficiency by taking a periodic inventory of the meetings we attend and asking questions about their productivity. Let's start with the meetings you yourself are in charge of.

- Are there meetings that are now being held regularly while resulting in few tangible benefits? In the future, could these meetings be scheduled only when they're needed?
- Are there meetings that serve primarily to exchange information instead of to debate issues and make decisions? Are there other ways of exchanging information that would be more efficient?
- Would it be more effective to have fewer but shorter, single-focus meetings—in which people get together, make a decision about one specific issue, and then disperse—rather than longer, multiple-focus meetings?
- Are there meetings that do not need to be held in person but could be done through teleconferencing, e-mail exchanges, phone calls, or other means?
- Do the meetings involve everyone who is required in order to make a decision and *only* them? If you're calling a meeting but it lacks some of the people who are necessary for the decision to be made, you're wasting people's time. Similarly, if there are people at the meeting who are not essential to the decisions that have to be made, you're wasting *their* time.

One quick way of calculating whether a particular meeting may be a black hole of time is to take (or estimate) the hourly wage of each person in attendance at the meeting, figure out the total salary investment the institution made to have that meeting, and then ask whether the results that came out of the meeting were worth that cost. In many cases, you'll discover that the cost/benefit ratio for the meeting is heavily out of balance on the cost side, suggesting that alternatives to holding the meeting should probably be explored.

Your options are more limited with regard to meetings that you yourself do not run but which you are required to attend. In these cases, if you consider your presence at a meeting to be unnecessary, you may want to talk to the person in charge about the possibility of changing the requirements for attendance. Sometimes the person will have the authority to make that decision on his or her own; sometimes bylaws or policies will need to be changed. But the investment of time in making these adjustments may pay off substantially in the long run through the additional amount of time you then have available for more productive work.

Another area in which black holes of time may occur is when we feel that our responsibilities pull us in different directions and prevent us from giving any of our duties the focus they truly deserve. For example, our teaching may pull us in one direction, our research in another, our committee work in a third, and our obligation to perform other administrative activities in a fourth direction. Compartmentalizing our responsibilities in this way can be a highly inefficient way to get things done. Each individual compartment then becomes its own black hole of time.

A more efficient approach would be to *leverage your time*. In other words, seek ways in which what you do in one aspect of your responsibilities can help you achieve important goals in at least one other area. If you make an administrative task also function as a research project, you may get better results in both areas.

Let's suppose one of your goals as an academic leader is to improve student success—which, for the purposes of this hypothetical example, we'll define as increased retention from lower-division to upper-division courses and improvement in your program's six-year graduation rate—and that you're finding this activity to be incredibly time-consuming. The lessons you learn from how peer and aspirational institutions have addressed these problems could become the basis for an article in a professional journal. And if you conduct an experiment—say, using one teaching technique in one section of a course but a different technique in another section—you may end up with results that you can present at a conference.

Or suppose you find that all the time you spend in committee meetings is distracting you from the time you really need to spend on other administrative tasks, such as engaging in outcomes assessment, program review, or strategic planning. It may be that the responsibilities of the committees on which you're serving are close enough to some of those administrative tasks that aspects of those projects can be performed as part of the committee's regular work. In this case, you will receive the added advantage of having helped transform an underproductive committee into a highly productive set of coworkers.

The last topic relating to black holes of time that we need to consider will take us into what some readers may regard as a slightly uncomfortable area: black holes of time that may exist in your personal life, not because you find them beneficial, but because of social pressure, tradition, or mere habit. Consider the sheer time investment involved in the following life activities:

- reading newspapers, watching the evening news, and otherwise keeping up with current events
- engaging in social media

- playing video games
- watching television and going to movies
- raising children
- participating in sports or attending athletic events
- being an active member in a church, mosque, synagogue, temple, or other center of religious activity
- being a member of a community service organization or country club
- caring for pets

Some people will examine this list and think, "He can't be suggesting that I give up my church! My spiritual life is central to who I am," or "How can you even suggest that I not raise a family? Caring for children isn't something I just do as a pastime. It's a vital part of my life."

In those cases, these activities aren't black holes of time for these people. They're rewarding and meaningful activities. But that's not true for everyone. Many people simply engage in religious rituals, settle down to raise a family, join the Rotary Club, watch football games, take care of a dog or cat, and do other items on this list because they think it's expected of them or because it's just become a habit.

We've probably all met at least one person who lives a happy, self-fulfilled life *without devoting time to any of the bulleted items on that list*. They're not religious. They don't have children. They don't pay attention to the news, join clubs, or go to athletic events, and yet they're happy. That's because they're not spending time on activities that are not rewarding for them (i.e., black holes of time) but instead are focusing their efforts on what truly matters to them, gives them joy, and produces results that they consider worthwhile.

As you scan that list of time-consuming personal activities, you're unlikely to find that you're one of those people who would be satisfied without doing *any* of the things mentioned there. But, as you reflect on it, you may find that there are one or two activities in your personal life for which the time investment is wholly disproportionate to the amount of happiness and satisfaction you receive from them. It's those activities that may be serving as black holes of time in your personal life, and if you can remove them—or even reduce the time you devote to them—you will be able to reinvest that time savings into other activities that bring you more rewarding results.

Chapter 11

Reprogramming Yourself

In the last chapter, we touched on the topic of doing things because they were habitual, not because they were rewarding or productive. In this chapter, we want to expand on this idea by considering how we can go about replacing bad habits with good habits and transforming unpleasant habits into more rewarding habits.

A great deal of research has been done about how habits are formed and how they can be replaced, including Charles Duhigg's *The Power of Habit* (2014) and *Smarter Faster Better: The Transformative Power of Real Productivity* (2017), Jeremy Dean's *Making Habits, Breaking Habits* (2013), and Richard O'Connor's *Rewire: Change Your Brain* (2015). So, if you want to replace time-consuming habits with, for example, Stephen Covey's seven habits of highly effective people (Covey, 1989) or Kevin Kruse's productivity habits of billionaires, Olympic athletes, straight A students, and entrepreneurs, what do you do?

The first step in changing a habit is understanding what a habit really is. A habit is simply an automatic or semiautomatic routine that a person can complete without much conscious thought. You know you're dealing with a habit when you find that you sometimes forget whether you've performed that activity.

For most of us, brushing our teeth or locking our cars is a habit. We perform these activities while we're often thinking about other things. And that's why we sometimes have to run our tongues across our teeth, searching for that clean feeling and minty taste, or go back to the car and check the door. Because our thoughts were elsewhere, we weren't creating memories of the activity.

The second step is understanding that it is extremely difficult to eliminate a habit once it has been created. Since we engage in the habit without much conscious thought, habits become activities that we perform on "autopilot" or with "muscle memory." The unconscious parts of our brains take over, and it becomes all but impossible for our conscious minds to overpower what our unconscious minds are used to doing. For this reason, we break bad habits by *replacing habits we don't want with newer habits we do want*.

Third, we need to understand the context in which our habits are performed. The typical habit cycle starts with a *cue* (an occurrence or situation that initiates the cycle), proceeds to the *routine* (the actual activity that we regard as the habit), and ends with a *reward* (a feeling that could extend anywhere from mild satisfaction to intense physical pleasure).

So, as we're leaving our cars, the physical action of opening the door and getting out of the vehicle is the cue. Locking the door is the routine, and the feeling of safety that results is the reward. If we don't notice the reward because our thoughts are preoccupied with other concerns, we're likely to forget whether the routine has occurred and go back to check.

Fourth, the most effective way to replace an old habit with a new one is to keep the cue and the reward but insert a new routine. That substitution will have to be done consciously at first, but eventually the new routine becomes automatic as well.

So, if we have a habit of eating unhealthy snacks when we sit down to watch our favorite programs, we change the routine by making it much more difficult to retrieve the unhealthy snacks by placing them in a high cupboard located in a distant room and imposing the artificial rule that we must now eat our snacks with a knife and fork. At the same time, we place a bowl of fruit or other healthy food nearer the television and allow ourselves to indulge in those foods without any artificial restrictions.

In time, it becomes more natural to reach over and grab an apple when we're hungry than climbing a flight of stairs, getting a step stool, opening a high cabinet, and then trying to eat our potato chips and candy bars with a knife and fork. The award will be the same or may now even be greater because we'll have the additional satisfaction of thinking, "I'm the sort of person who eats healthy food."

Fifth, habits are easiest to replace when we attempt to address only one habit at a time. If we try to change all of our bad or time-consuming habits at once, we're likely to find ourselves overwhelmed by the amount of effort required and give up.

Charles Duhigg recommends trying to identify what he calls a *keystone habit*: a single activity that may launch other dependent habits (see Duhigg, 2014, 97–126). For example, when we come into our offices in the morning, the first thing we do may be to turn on our computers. That habit then leads us to check our e-mail, which may then lead us to call someone back to follow-up on an action required by something he or she wrote us about or by engaging in an activity that now seems urgent rather than important. (See chapter 3 on this distinction.)

If that habit is proving to be productive for you, then it's fine; there's no need to change it. But if your personal energy cycle (see chapter 5) suggests that the first thing in the morning is the best time for you to engage in your research or perform some other activity of high importance, then a better alternative is to spend half an hour or so on that activity before turning your computer on (or at least before opening your e-mail) each day.

The feeling of satisfaction and progress that results from your increased productivity may well lead to more efficient habits elsewhere in your work. That simple change of not answering e-mails first thing in the day will be the keystone habit that alters your self-image from a person who is constantly burdened by overwork to a person who gets important work done in a timely manner.

Sixth, we need to understand the *obstacles* (Duhigg calls them *inflection points*; Duhigg, 2014, 143–147) that cause us to give up in our efforts to replace old habits with new ones and develop preplanned routines to overcome those obstacles. An obstacle might be that colleague who regularly shows up in your doorway, engages in unproductive conversation, and takes a long time to leave. Since you recognize this colleague as an obstacle to your productivity, you can develop a strategy for dealing with his or her interruptions. That strategy might be saying something like, "I'd love to continue this conversation, but I'm swamped right now and have a report to complete within the next hour. Can we go to lunch together and catch up?"

Seventh, we have to allow enough time for our new habit to become part of our standard operating procedure. For many years, books on time management and habit formation used to say that it takes twenty-one days for a new habit to become routine.

But Jeremy Dean has convincingly refuted that notion, tracing its origin to a single study by Maxwell Maltz on how long it generally takes amputees to adjust to the loss of a limb. Dean's own research has indicated that, although simple habits (such as remembering to drink a glass of water immediately after getting up in the morning) can often be formed within three weeks, truly complex habits take at least sixty-six days (and often as long as twelve full weeks) to become automatic.

So, don't give up if a month goes by and you're still tempted to engage in unproductive routines. You may need to make a conscious effort at reprogramming yourself for a full semester before you notice that you're working more productively without having to think about it.

A particularly common bad habit that administrators get into in higher education is what is known as *thriving on busy*. You'll recognize someone—perhaps yourself—who has developed this habit because his or her typical answer to the question "How are you today?" is "Busy!" Thriving on busy occurs when people have developed the habit of seeing activity as rewarding for its own sake. In other words, the cue is arriving at work, the routine is frantic activity, and the reward is a sense of importance because "I'm a busy person."

In my own executive coaching of academic leaders, I've urged those who indulge in thriving on busy to make just one easy change: Instead of answering "Busy!" when asked how they are, the administrators are restricted to respond by saying, "I'm getting so much done!" or "I'm crossing items off my to-do list left and right!"

That reply seems a bit artificial at first, but it gradually changes the person's self-image and routine. Academic leaders start seeing themselves not as someone who's overwhelmed with work but as someone who's highly productive. Their subconscious minds then begin rewarding them with satisfaction not for being busy but for *getting things done*. Almost inevitably, the administrator will tell me in a follow-up conversation how that one easy change produced a dramatic increase in his or her time efficiency.

Another small change one can make that results in a disproportionate increase in productivity is the *one-touch method*. With this method, you don't allow an entire day to go by without making at least one minor bit of progress on a long-term project.

As an example, when writing an article, your one touch for a day might be as significant as writing ten pages of your final draft or as small as looking up a single item for your literature review. In a curriculum revision, your one touch could range from making a formal presentation to the faculty senate down to checking out the website of a similar program at another university.

The important requirement is that you do *something* every day. In this way, the project remains active in our minds, and we're less likely to let important deadlines slip through the cracks.

The final approach to reprogramming yourself that we want to explore in this chapter comes from an unlikely source: the 1964 Walt Disney film *Mary Poppins*. The title character in that movie is trying to encourage the Banks children to do their chores and tells them, "In every job that must be done, there is an element of fun. You find the fun, and—snap! The job's a game."

That advice can actually work with many of those tedious or unpleasant tasks we have to do as academic leaders. Writing a lengthy series of faculty evaluations is certainly important, but it can be incredibly dull. Meeting with a faculty member who's upset with his or her course assignment is significant, but it can be very unpleasant.

But if an academic leader tries to identify an element of fun or challenge in these activities, they become much more enjoyable. "Let's see if I can write this entire evaluation, make it extremely positive, but avoid using the words *good*, *excellent*, or *outstanding* in the entire document." "Professor Curmudgeon is coming in to complain about his course assignment today. Maybe I should approach this meeting more as an anthropologist than merely as an administrator and try to understand the cultural values that 'make Professor Curmudgeon tick.'"

The idea is thus to find a way to enjoy those tasks that you're going to have to do anyway. By doing so, you'll stop putting them off, get them out of the way, and be able to move on to other productive activities.

Many authors who discuss techniques for changing habits and reprogramming oneself so as to be more productive devote a great deal of attention to the practice of *mindfulness meditation* as a means of restructuring how one approaches events that are usually regarded as unpleasant or disagreeable (see, for instance, O'Connor, 2015, 69–72 and 206–239.) In fact, many people who engage in an active practice of mindfulness meditation find that they receive a dual benefit: In addition to being able to focus on more of their high-priority objectives, they also find themselves feeling calmer and less stressed.

To be sure, as we've seen repeatedly, time management and stress management are almost impossible to pursue independently. If we wish to be in a position to cope with the stress of our jobs, we have to get our "time management house" in order, and, if we wish to manage our time effectively, we can't become consumed by anxieties that distract us from our priorities.

So, now that we have done so by exploring in chapters 2 through 11 the ten most productive time management techniques I know, we are ready to turn our attention to the second great challenge of academic leaders: dealing with all the stress that arises because of their responsibilities and the effect their decisions have on others.

Part II

MANAGING YOUR STRESS

Chapter 12

The Origins of Administrative Stress

From everything we hear on the news, we're likely to conclude that stress is a horrible thing that produces absolutely no benefits and that we ought to eliminate stress from our lives as much as possible. But that really isn't the case. There's both good stress and bad stress. To understand why that's the case, we first need to review what stress really is.

Stress is your *body's natural response to any perceived threat*. There are two key words in that definition. First, stress is *natural*. In other words, it has survival value. Back when human beings were hunter-gatherers, the sudden appearance of a wild boar created a truly dangerous situation. Anyone who didn't respond quickly might be killed (and thus removed from the gene pool).

Those who had a strong *fight-or-flight response*, as the physiologist Walter Cannon first termed it, had a far better chance of survival. They either attacked the wild boar immediately, killing it or driving it off, or ran away to fight another day. In either case, their stress—the sudden adrenaline rush that caused their strong reaction—saved their lives and increased the likelihood that their genes would be passed on to subsequent generations.

The second key word in our definition of stress is *perceived*. No matter whether the threat is actual (a real wild boar emerging from the bushes) or imagined (a shadow on a log that is mistaken for a wild boar), a person's body responds in exactly the same way. That's why a response that once was life-preserving has turned life-compromising today. The sorts of things that cause stress for most academic leaders—those tight deadlines and demanding stakeholders—don't really threaten their *lives* any longer, but their bodies respond just the same.

The problem is that wild boars were rare threats. The types of experiences that our bodies experience in academic leadership roles today are daily, almost continual "threats." For this reason, we don't have the recovery time our bodies need to process and reabsorb the stress hormones associated with the last time we experienced a fight-or-flight response. We remain in a state of *perpetual unresolved stress*, and that condition causes all the detrimental effects of stress that we explored earlier.

A common sign that you're in a state of perpetual unresolved stress is that you're able to fall asleep at night but unable to remain asleep. At some point, often between 2:00 a.m. and 4:00 a.m., you wake up, feel alert to the point of being anxious, and can only go to sleep again with great difficulty if at all. What's happened is that your body is responding to an influx of *cortisol*, the steroid hormone that your body produces to prepare you to become alert the next day.

Usually, the small amount of cortisol our bodies release doesn't cause us any problem. It allows us to wake up refreshed the next morning and have the energy we need to start the day. But if we're under a lot of unresolved stress, all the adrenaline we still have in our system, combined with the shock of additional cortisol, produces the effect where we wake up suddenly anxious, even if we can't figure out exactly what we're anxious about.

Some people say that this cortisol effect causes them to sit up suddenly in bed. Others say it feels as though every cell in their body were tingling. Still others say that they merely feel alert and generally depressed or worried. The specific response you have depends on many factors, but the cause is the same: perpetual unresolved stress.

So, how much stress are you under these days? To try to determine how much of an issue stress is for you, Table 12.1 shows a simple inventory. Read each statement carefully, and then respond whether the statement applies to you always, often, sometimes, rarely, or never. After you complete the inventory, you'll be told how to calculate your score.

Table 12.1 General Stress Inventory

	Never (1)	Rarely (2)	Sometimes (3)	Often (4)	Always (5)
1. I care more deeply about things than do other people.					
2. When I do something, I try to do it perfectly.					
3. I wake up at night and can't go back to sleep for an hour or more.					

4. I think about poor decisions I've made in the past and wish I could undo them.					
5. People tell me that I have a forceful personality.					
6. Those who know me well or work with me say that I'm moody.					
7. When I get home after a day's work, I'm exhausted.					
8. I worry about making mistakes, disappointing others, or making people angry at me.					
9. My muscles become sore because they tense up.					
10. When the pressure's on, I find myself almost paralyzed; I have difficulty deciding what to do next.					
11. To handle pressure, I smoke, drink, or turn to comfort foods.					
12. I tend to increase the number of my activities when I am under pressure or feeling anxious.					
13. I find myself becoming angry at work.					
14. I suffer from "intestinal distress" that doesn't appear to be food-related.					
15. I find it difficult to set work aside when on vacation.					

After you've completed the inventory, score 1 point for each time you've checked the box marked *Never (1)*, 2 points for *Rarely (2)*, 3 points for *Sometimes (3)*, 4 points for *Often (4)*, and 5 points for *Always (5)*. When you add these numbers together, your score should thus be at least 15 and no greater than 75.

You can then interpret this score according to the following scale:

If your score falls in the range of *15–35*, you're either not under a great deal of stress or you're handling it well. The ideas that we'll explore in this book may represent a great deal of what you're already doing, or you might use these ideas to help other people who are experiencing stress in your program. You yourself, however, are not being adversely affected by work-related stress.

If your score falls in the range of *36–55*, you're in the category where most academic leaders find themselves. Stress is not really debilitating for you, but it does sometimes affect your work, and it may also be affecting your health. Consider the strategies that we'll explore throughout the following chapters, and select those that seem most likely to be useful for the way you work and that fit your lifestyle.

If your score falls in the range of 56–75, you're experiencing a high level of stress and not dealing with it very effectively. In fact, stress may already be having an adverse effect on your health. In addition to considering the strategies that we'll explore in this book, you may want to mention to your doctor that you seem to have difficulty dealing with the amount of stress that you're experiencing. Your doctor may want to conduct certain tests or keep an eye on certain factors to make sure that the negative impact of stress on your health is reduced as much as possible.

MORE ON GOOD VERSUS BAD STRESS

Although few of us these days are likely to encounter a wild boar, there are still ways in which a certain amount of stress can actually be helpful. That adrenaline rush when we're under pressure can spur us to do our best work, meet tight deadlines, and overcome our inertia. In fact, for most academic leaders, a little bit of stress is probably better than no stress at all. In a completely depressurized environment, our programs tend to stagnate. There simply aren't sufficient incentives for us to make something great as long as it's already "pretty good."

In fact, stressful environments, at times, may inspire achievements that wouldn't have been possible if matters had been calm. There's a famous scene in the 1949 film *The Third Man* in which Harry Lime (played by Orson Welles) tries to cheer up his old friend Holly Martins (Joseph Cotton) by making this very point:

> Don't be so gloomy. After all it's not that awful. Like the fella says, in Italy for thirty years under the Borgias they had warfare, terror, murder, and bloodshed, but they produced Michelangelo, Leonardo da Vinci, and the Renaissance. In Switzerland they had brotherly love—500 years of democracy and peace—and what did that produce? The cuckoo clock.

While too much stress can be destructive, too little stress can be boring, enervating, and stultifying. The big question is "How much stress is the right amount?" and that question can vary a great deal from person to person. We might think of stress, therefore, as something like a violin string. If the string is too tight, it snaps. If it's too loose, no sound is possible. But if it's tuned just tight enough, a wonderful melody can result.

It's rarely the case, then, that any of us will flourish in an environment where we experience absolutely no pressure. Instead, we're likely to find our performance affected by stress similar to what is depicted in Figure 12.1: The quality of our work improves a little bit as our stress level increases, but

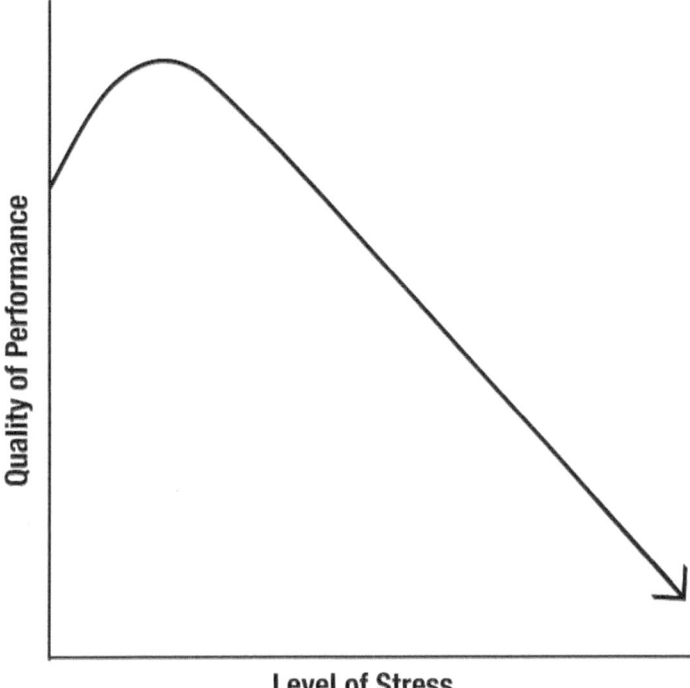

Figure 12.1

returns quickly diminish, and after a certain point, the more stress we have, the more our performance declines.

The tricky part is to determine the right level of stress for each of us. In order to get a general sense of the work-related stress level that's right for you, we'll conduct another inventory. As in the General Stress Inventory, read each statement in Table 12.2 carefully and check one of the boxes. But this time, rather than indicating how often you act in the way described, respond by reporting how well the statement describes you:

- This statement sounds *exactly* like me.
- This statement sounds like me *much of the time*.
- This statement sounds like me *occasionally*.
- This statement sounds *nothing* like me.

Once again, after you complete the inventory, you'll be told how to calculate your score.

Table 12.2 Excitement Tolerance Inventory

	Exactly Like Me (4)	Like Me Much of the Time (3)	Like Me Occasionally (2)	Nothing Like Me (1)
1. I do my best work when an imminent deadline is looming.				
2. Skydiving and rollercoasters fascinate me.				
3. I enjoy reading suspense novels or going to horror films.				
4. I'd prefer taking a trip with no plan in mind at all to one that is carefully planned to the last detail.				
5. I love surprises: Make me the guest of honor at a surprise party anytime.				
6. Given the choice, I'd rather have excitement in my life than serenity.				
7. My favorite social events are those when I'm never quite sure what will happen.				
8. The sports or hobbies I like best always seem to have some element of danger in them.				
9. I'm at my best in a crisis.				
10. I like to think of myself as something of a gambler or risk-taker.				

Total your score by giving yourself 1 point for each time you checked the box marked *Nothing Like Me (1)*, 2 points for *Like Me Occasionally (2)*, 3 points for *Like Me Most of the Time (3)*, and 4 points for *Exactly Like Me (4)*. When you add these numbers together, your score should be at least 10 and no greater than 40.

If your score falls in the range of *10–20*, you have a very low tolerance for stress. Highly pressurized situations probably make you nervous, and you're unlikely to make your best decisions at that time. You'll want to be proactive in eliminating stress before it arises instead of just reducing stress once it has already occurred. For this reason, you'll want to pay particular attention to chapter 14, which deals directly with effective practices for stress reduction.

If your score falls in the range of *21–30*, you fall in the midrange for stress tolerance. You like a little excitement in your life but not constantly. In many ways, people who fall in this category have the most challenging stress management issues. They tend not to seek professions and lifestyles that are completely tranquil and stress-free; they'd quickly find these options boring. But they also tend to avoid high-pressured careers, such as stockbroker or air traffic controller, because the never-ending stress of that work would be too much for them.

Many academic leaders fall in this category because they're attracted to the low-stress environment that a scholarly life promises, but they then find themselves in more highly pressurized positions as academic leaders. If you fall into this category, your most successful approach might be to combine some of the suggestions from chapters 13 through 16, developing your own customized approach to dealing with job-related stress.

If your score falls in the range of *31–40*, you have a relatively high threshold for stress. Situations that may seem unbearably tense for others may sometimes seem exciting or thrilling to you. When stress does affect you negatively, however, you may find some of the suggestions explored in chapter 13, which explores the concept of embracing stress, to be most helpful.

FIRST STEPS TOWARD DEALING WITH STRESS

If too much stress can have harmful effects on your health, not paying enough attention to your health can also increase your stress. So, although it may seem obvious, it's important to note that you're unlikely to be able to deal with stress effectively if you don't

- eat a good diet,
- exercise regularly, and
- get a full night's sleep.

We might call these three guidelines our *healthful living prerequisites for dealing with stress*. If we fail to fulfill those prerequisites, it can be difficult or even impossible to make much progress in handling the pressures of our jobs.

For some people, that advice can seem a bit paradoxical. They might say things like, "But stress is exactly what makes me favor comfort food over more healthy options/feel too exhausted to even think about getting more exercise/unable to sleep through the entire night. How can you recommend these steps as prerequisites for effective stress management when I first need effective stress management in order to do them?" That's not at all an unfair question, and it's why chapter 17 is dedicated to the topic of comprehensive approaches to managing time and stress or, as we'll call it, dealing with time and stress holistically.

For now, however, the best way for you to begin the process of dealing with the stress of being an academic leader is to establish a clear intention of handling the pressure of your job better. Though stress may tempt you to favor pot roast or ice cream over fresh vegetables, set the intention of eating more healthy foods. If you rid your pantry of the sorts of snacks you're trying to avoid, it'll be easier for you to sidestep temptation when stressful situations arise.

In a similar way, use your calendar to schedule regular appointments with yourself for a vigorous walk or a trip to the gym even if you sometimes have to break those appointments. You're more likely to get exercise if you schedule it, set a firm intention of honoring that schedule, and mention that intention to others than if all you do is merely *think* that getting more exercise would be a good thing.

Go to bed early enough that you *could* get a good night's sleep, even if you end up falling asleep much later or waking up sometime during the night. You have no chance at all of getting eight hours of rest if you don't go to bed until after midnight and have to be up by 6:00 a.m. It can be frustrating to lie awake for hours on end—or what will only seem like hours on end—but you may also find that, if you keep to this plan, you do start to sleep more deeply and consistently after a few weeks.

In short, if you find that you're so stressed that you simply can't fulfill the three healthful living prerequisites for dealing with stress listed earlier, at least create the appropriate conditions that would make those prerequisites possible at some point. Then, as you follow the advice outlined in the rest of this book, you may discover that, at some point, you actually *are* eating better, exercising more regularly, and sleeping longer.

YOUR PERSONAL STRESS INVENTORY

We have one last step to complete before we can start exploring the specific ways in which you can deal with stress more effectively. We first need to conduct a candid self-assessment of the things that cause us stress. Anything that raises a person's stress level is designated a *trigger* for that person. And triggers can be very personal. What causes your blood pressure to rise and heart to race may have little or no effect on your colleague. So, in order for you to know exactly what to do in the chapters that follow, you have to complete an inventory of the various triggers you have in your life.

Triggers are generally of two kinds: predisposing and precipitating. You can think of a *predisposing trigger* as each individual straw added to a camel's load. A *precipitating trigger*, on the other hand, is the proverbial straw that breaks the camel's back: the one thing that, without fail, puts you over the edge into a highly stressed state or, in the most severe of cases, prompts a panic attack.

You may or may not be aware of the predisposing triggers as they occur, but you (and probably everyone around you) are most definitely aware of the precipitating triggers. You can think of a precipitating trigger as a statement or event that causes a significant or dramatic response from you that can seem baffling because the severity of your reaction appears disproportionate to the incident itself, until you recall all the predisposing triggers that led up to that reaction.

With this framework in mind, let's begin to identify the predisposing and precipitating triggers that tend to affect you in your life and work. Before moving on to the next chapter, try to identify at least five triggers of each kind, and write your responses in Table 12.3.

For your list of predisposing triggers, try to think of general circumstances that you already know increase your stress level. For example, do you find yourself feeling under more pressure during the academic year than in the summer? Many academic leaders do, but not many of them reflect on exactly what's different about the academic year that sets it apart from the summer. For some, it may be that the academic year has more tight deadlines. For other academic leaders, it may be that there are more students on campus, which tends to cause more stress for faculty members, which in turn causes more stress for administrators.

If you can't identify your predisposing triggers in any other way, go back in your mind to the last time you recall feeling reasonably free from stress at work. What was different about what was going on at that point in time from what's going on in your work environment now?

For your list of precipitating triggers, think of the times when someone did or said something that, for whatever reason, "put you over the edge" and

Table 12.3 Predisposing and Precipitating Triggers

Predisposing Triggers	Precipitating Triggers
1.	1.
2.	2.
3.	3.
4.	4.
5.	5.

increased your stress level tremendously. There were probably many predisposing triggers that led up to that moment, but see if you can identify what it was precisely that intensified the stress you were under. Did it matter more *who* said or did the precipitating factor, the *attitude* with which it was said or done, the *timing* at which it occurred, or some other aspect of the experience that was important to you?

Now that you've completed the three inventories presented in Tables 12.1, 12.2, and 12.3—the amount of stress you're under and how you're handling it, your personal preference for excitement and tolerance for stress, and your lists of predisposing and precipitating triggers for stress—we can begin to use these results as part of a comprehensive approach to deal with the pressures of academic leadership more effectively.

No single approach to work-related stress is the best solution for everyone, so we're going to consider a wide number of options from which you can pick and choose. In order to make it easier to combine several options into your own holistic approach to dealing with stress, we'll group these techniques into four categories based on the overall strategies they use:

- embracing stress,
- reducing stress,
- managing stress, and
- coping with stress.

Chapter 13

Embracing Stress

The first approach to dealing with stress that we'll consider is one that most people are likely to regard as very innovative, perhaps even a bit strange, but it actually has a rather distinguished history. Although the *Oxford English Dictionary* cites examples of the word *stress* applied to people and their circumstances as early as the beginning of the fourteenth century, for more than 600 years, a great deal more was known about the effect of stress on physical materials, like stone and iron, than on human beings.

That situation began to change dramatically through the work of one individual: the Austro-Hungarian-Canadian endocrinologist Hans Selye (pronounced: SELL-ya). Selye theorized that humans, like other animals, experienced something that he called the general adaptation syndrome. This syndrome, Selye argued, had three distinct stages.

Stage One: Alarm. A trigger occurs, and the body's limbic system (the brain's system of nerves and networks where most of our emotional reactions occur) responds. It's during the stage of alarm that Cannon's fight-or-flight response begins. Blood pressure rises. Heartbeat quickens. Adrenaline and cortisol are released.

Stage Two: Resistance. The adrenaline and cortisol in the body increase the concentration of sugar, fat, and amino acids in the bloodstream. The person is then chemically equipped to resist the trigger: Basically his or her body is now prepared for fight or flight.

Stage Three: Either Recovery or Exhaustion. If the trigger is successfully "disarmed," the threat passes, and the body recovers to its ordinary stage. But if the trigger can't be disarmed, the stress continues until the body's hormonal and other chemical resources are depleted, resulting in exhaustion. It's this state of exhaustion that, Selye believed, resulted in the physical damage produced by stress and that he sought to address through his recommendations on how to deal with the stress-producing conditions of life.

We can think of the general adaptation syndrome in this way: Imagine that you're driving down the freeway when, suddenly, a state patrol car behind you turns on its lights and siren. What you see and hear is a trigger that leads to a state of alarm. The tension, worry, and panic you feel are the resistance your body produces in order to deal with that alarm.

Suppose then that the patrol car suddenly pulls around you and begins to pursue a car in a lane beside you. You might almost immediately feel the tension leave your body and sense that everything's returned to normal. Within a surprisingly short time, you're feeling just as relaxed as you were before you heard the siren and noticed the lights in your rearview mirror. You've entered the stage of recovery.

But suppose the situation were to go a different way. The officer pulls you over, lectures you about putting other people's lives in jeopardy because of the way you were driving, and gives you a ticket that will require a court appearance and almost certainly lead to a significant fine.

The delay caused by this traffic stop makes you late for a meeting where you now have to deal with several angry faculty members who feel you've wasted their time. When you get out of the meeting, your supervisor tells you that she or he has been trying to reach you for the past hour and needs you to set everything else aside so that you can complete a long, detailed report by the end of the day. Meeting your boss's expectations then makes you late getting home that night where you find that your partner is upset with you because you've forgotten today is your anniversary.

In the latter scenario, your body will probably never reach the state of recovery before a new trigger causes you to revisit the stages of alarm and resistance. You'll exhaust every resource you have for dealing with this stress and probably end up in anger, tears, or both, which may actually make the situation worse and leave you feeling even more stress.

THE CONCEPT OF EUSTRESS

Selye noted that these negative sensations that we feel in such a situation and that we generally call *stress* are actually better regarded as signs of *distress*, a term usually used to refer to anxiety, pain, and worry. But Selye recognized that many of the same physical reactions that our bodies undergo during the general adaptation syndrome—such as an increase in blood pressure, a more rapid heartbeat, and the release of adrenaline and cortisol—also occur during *joyful* experiences, such as when we're getting married, receiving public recognition, or being offered a promotion.

In fact, as we saw earlier in this book, some people actually *expose* themselves to experiences that others would regard as highly stressful. They go skydiving, attend scary movies, engage in extreme sports, and the like. In other words, there are certain activities that, at least for certain personality types, are *both stressful and pleasant simultaneously*.

Selye argued that, if we could learn what made stress triggers positive experiences for some and negative experiences for others—or if we could determine what distinguished our own joyful moments of stress from our unpleasant moments of stress—then we would have an important mechanism for helping us deal more effectively with the pressures of work and everyday life.

The basic idea is that, if we could cause ourselves to reinterpret *stress* as *excitement*, we could deal with it better. So, what really are the differences between going to a tense and frightening meeting with your boss and going to a tense and frightening movie with your friends? Two differences really stand out:

- You *choose* to go to the movie. You *have* to go see your boss.
- No matter how scary the movie is, you know you'll be *safe* at the end. In the meeting with your boss, you could suffer some serious *detriment* (e.g., to career, income, or ego) by the end.

Those two differences—the amount of control we feel we have over the situation and whether we have a reasonable expectation of safety—matter a great deal.

They even explain why certain activities, such as skydiving and extreme sports, might be exciting for my friends but unbearably stressful to me. My friends are experienced and trained enough to know that they have a reasonable expectation of safety in those activities. They know that people are injured and even killed when engaging in these pastimes, but they know that those numbers are extremely low and almost infinitesimal with the right training, practice, and preparation. And so, they willingly choose to engage in these activities.

I, on the other hand, am not experienced or trained enough to have a reasonable expectation of safety while skydiving or engaging in extreme sports. Even if the chance of being hurt were only one in a billion, my mind is the sort that focuses on the one, not the billion. My reluctance to put myself at risk in these ways makes me feel as though I have very little control over the situation, while my friends are constantly urging me to "just try it once." Without control and expectation of safety, I'm stressed. With control and expectation of safety, they're excited.

That insight thus gives us our first practical strategy for dealing with the stress of academic leadership: When we find ourselves in highly pressurized situations, we need to look for *what control we have* and *how much safety still exists*. If we go back to the example of a tense and frightening meeting with your boss, what might we do to transform the stress of the situation into excitement?

Let's start with the issue of safety. When "called on the carpet" by your supervisor, your mind may easily jump to extreme scenarios such as, "Am I being fired?" or "Does this mean I'll be stripped of my administrative position?" But, when you think about the situation objectively, is that at all likely in this case?

Most of the time, it's not. Despite the stereotype of the blustering boss who likes nothing more than firing people for the slightest misstep or infraction, most supervisors in higher education aren't really like that. They may become upset with us from time to time. They may even raise their voices. But they're almost certainly not really going to fire us. Having to replace you would mean a great deal of work for your boss: finding a replacement, making the transition, getting the person prepared for the job, and so on. And there are hurdles from human resources to get past. Firing you would be a real hassle.

Moreover, have *you* ever had to fire someone? It's an anxiety-producing, unpleasant business. Your boss may well consider terminating you to be an even more unpleasant alternative than you do. (And that alone is an important insight to have: If you're stressed out about this meeting, your supervisor may be even *more* stressed out.) So, your job is probably safe, which means that *you're* safe.

And even if a worst-case scenario actually occurs and you *are* fired or forced to step down from your leadership position, you'd *still* be safe. Your family will still love you, and your credentials are good enough that you could get a new job if you wanted. All you'd be losing is the hassle of doing the parts of your job that you don't like anyway—like coming to this meeting with your boss that you've been dreading.

In addition to safety, you've got more *control* than you may realize. If your boss is truly abusive to you, your human resources department or an employment law attorney are available to protect you. If your professionalism is impugned, you know that you're enough of a professional to be assertive without being aggressive.

In fact, you may be able to turn a tense meeting into something highly beneficial for your program. Is your supervisor angry because a report was late or poorly done? You can attribute that to being understaffed and request a new assistant. Is your supervisor upset because you weren't publicly supportive of his or her latest initiative? The meeting can become your opportunity to explain, clearly and in detail, why that initiative in its current form is harmful to your program and needs to be revised.

In other words, your control comes from realizing that you have many more options than simply sitting there, taking your boss's abuse, and feeling miserable. You have both safety and control, which means that you can start to feel less stressed and more excited about the situation. And although this type of reinterpretation won't work for all the triggers of your stress, when you begin to experiment with this approach, you'll find that it's effective in more situations than you may initially expect.

EUSTRESS

Since Selye observed that the kind of stress that actually concerns us is really *dis*tress, he wanted to coin a term that could be used for the more positive form of stress that we have when we're excited. For this purpose, Selye proposed the term *eustress*, adopting the Greek prefix *eu-* meaning *good*, *well*, or *pleasant* that appears in such words as *eulogy* (remarks that "speak well" of a deceased person) and *euphonious* (an adjective applied to "pleasant sounds" as opposed to noise or cacophony).

Etymologically, Selye's term is kind of a muddle. The Latin prefix *dis-* actually means *apart or away* from, as in *disbar* (sending someone *away* from the legal *bar*), *discontent* (being *apart from content*), and *disagreement* (what people have when they're *away from agreement*).

The word *distress* has a rather complicated development from late Latin through French to English, but the one thing that it doesn't have is the Greek prefix *dys-* (meaning *bad*, *poor*, or *harmful*), which shows up in such words as *dysfunctional* (an adjective applied to things that *function poorly*), *dyspepsia* (a state of *bad digestion*), or *dystrophy* (the condition of muscles and organs that are *poorly nourished* or that *develop poorly*).

The prefix *eu-* is a logical counterpart to *dys-*, not *dis-*. So, what Selye did was counter a Latin prefix (*dis-*) with a Greek prefix (*eu-*) that wasn't really its logical opposite. Nevertheless, the coinage caught on, and the word *eustress* is now commonly used to describe a reasonable amount of stress that is beneficial to or pleasant for the person experiencing it.

Quibbles about etymology aside, there are a number of proven ways to try to transform stress into excitement or distress into eustress. In fact, the clinical psychologist Melanie Greenberg has identified six such ways:

1. *Find Meaning in the Situation.* Reflect on what you're learning from the stressful situation and how you're growing as a person. Ask yourself, "How will I be better or stronger for having experienced this?"
2. *Adopt a Growth Mind-set.* Remind yourself that you're not a helpless victim of circumstance. You've been in highly pressurized situations before, developed the skills you needed to deal with them, and survived. Ask yourself, "How could this challenge be a learning opportunity? What chance does it provide to develop new areas of expertise?"

3. *Find Support*. Remember that you're not alone, no matter how lonely the current situation may feel. There are always other people in your family or peer group who can support you, advise you, and remind you how much they're on your side. Ask yourself, "Who can help me flourish in the face of this current challenge?"
4. *Practice Mindfulness*. Meditation, deep breathing exercises, stretching, and yoga (all of which we'll examine further in chapter 15) can all help you feel more grounded in the present moment instead of caught up in worries about the future. With mindfulness, you don't try to escape the stressful situation by ignoring it. Rather, it helps you see the situation within a larger and more balanced context. Ask yourself, "What am I experiencing right now?" as opposed to "What am I afraid might happen later?"
5. *Break the Problem Down into Manageable Steps*. Some situations are stressful because we don't know where to begin. In a reversal of the familiar "can't see the forest for the trees," we feel anxious because all we can see is one huge, seemingly impenetrable forest. But if we pause for a moment, as it were, to break the forest into a series of groves and one of the groves into a few identifiable clusters of trees and then identify one of those trees with which to begin, we can sometimes transform a project that initially appeared far too massive into a challenge that seems manageable, even perhaps fun. We can move from thinking, "Oh, no! That accreditation report is due in less than two weeks! That's impossible!" to thinking, "But maybe I could start by seeing how other universities did theirs," and finally to thinking, "You know, it would be kind of interesting to look at what Midlevel State University did with their report." So, when facing a task that feels overwhelming, ask yourself, "What's one small piece of this project that I can do right now?" or "How is this challenge similar to one that I've overcome before?"
6. *Imagine a Positive Future Self*. Stressful situations can paralyze us because we can only imagine the current difficult problem and not the ultimate benefit that will result from solving it. If we imagine ourselves basking in the glow of our success after we've emerged from the pressure we're under right now, that feeling of anticipatory relief can be enough of an incentive to get us moving toward actually correcting the situation, not simply worrying about it. Ask yourself, "How will I feel when I've fixed this problem and achieved an important goal?"

(For Greenberg's own, more complete discussion of her six-step approach to eustress, see Greenberg, 2014.)

LEANING IN TO STRESS

An important aspect of eustress is the notion that, paradoxically, the more we try to avoid or suppress the anxieties that arise in our professional lives, the larger we make them seem. It's an experience you've probably had when you were avoiding some looming task, convinced that it would be dull, difficult, or extremely time-consuming, only to discover that, once you actually began doing it, it wasn't so bad after all.

Much of what causes us stress functions in the same way: It's not really the trigger itself that causes us apprehension and discomfort, it's our fear that the activity will be far worse than it actually turns out to be. For this reason, one productive strategy for dealing with stress is *leaning in to it* any time we can feel ourselves tempted to avoid it. Get the stress-producing activity under way—even if you have to tell yourself that you just want to get it over with—and devote your energy to fully engaging in the activity, not wishing it away. Use the following slogan as your guide:

> If You Can't Get Out of It, Get Into It

As unexpected as it may be, approaching the situation in this way usually defuses the stress. Even more unexpectedly, you may find yourself *enjoying* the very activity you were dreading. Let's imagine, for a moment, that you have to make a presentation about a highly controversial proposal before your institution's governing board. You know that there are members of this board who are argumentative and thus object to almost anything brought before the group. But the proposal you're presenting is so divisive, it's likely to attract even more opposition than usual.

The very prospect of creating this presentation is making you anxious. You ask one of your colleagues for advice and are told, "Oh, just try not to think about it. Go about your work and do everything you need to do. There's no way you can make the board happy; the members are who they are. So, why worry about it now? Just deal with it when you get there."

If you try to follow this advice, the result is likely to be the opposite of what you were hoping for. It's almost impossible to put something out of your mind through willpower alone. As a result, the more you try not to think about it, the more the inevitability of that presentation will intrude on your thoughts. You'll find your anxiety level increasing. You won't be able to concentrate on your other work. That sense of unease will be apparent during the presentation itself, and the board members, feeling that you yourself are uncertain about the proposal, will be even more aggressive in their objections. You'll have made the situation worse instead of better.

But suppose you tried the opposite approach: *leaning in* to the anxiety-producing event. You might start out by thinking, "It's going to be nerve-racking no matter what I do, so I may as well get it over with." You might start to think of your presentation to the board as almost an anthropological study. What is it about the members that make them so argumentative? Which of them is likely to give me the greatest resistance, and what are those people most likely to resist? Will there be anyone on the board who will be more sympathetic to my ideas, and what can I do to encourage that person to support them publicly?

By leaning in to the situation, you've transformed a potentially tension-filled activity into a potentially interesting one. But as you continue this process, you can carry that transformation even further. Seeing the presentation as an anthropological or sociological study of the board members and their personalities makes it more about *them* than about *you*.

As an interested observer of the board's internal dynamics rather than a helpless recipient of their rancor, you've mentally removed yourself from the situation to the point where you start to believe that the presentation might actually be a bit enjoyable. After all, their argumentativeness isn't about you; it would be directed toward anyone. So, you find that you're starting to relax about the event and perhaps even begin to look forward to it.

When you go into the presentation, therefore, you'll probably be far more confident than you would've been otherwise. Your confidence could make your remarks seem more persuasive, and so, rather than attacking you as you had originally feared, most of the board members engage with you in an intense and interesting conversation about the proposal. You come out of the meeting thinking not just, "That wasn't so bad" but also "That was sort of fun."

In 1997, Mary Schmich, a columnist for *The Chicago Tribune*, made an observation that has since been falsely attributed to Eleanor Roosevelt, Kurt Vonnegut, and many others: "Do one thing every day that scares you." While it might be asking a bit much to make this type of eustress a *daily* activity, it's not bad advice when done periodically. By engaging in those activities that initially seem anxiety-producing to us, we widen our comfort zones and ultimately deal more effectively with the stress our jobs produce.

FOCUS ON PERSONAL AND PROFESSIONAL GROWTH

As we saw, one of Melanie Greenberg's ideas for turning distress into eustress was to adopt a growth mind-set. In doing so, she is adopting the vocabulary popularized by Carol Dweck in *Mindset: The New Psychology of Success*. Dweck's idea is that people largely rely on one of two primary mind-sets:

a *fixed mind-set* that views intelligence and other abilities as commodities ("You either have them or you don't.") or a *growth mind-set* that views intelligence and other abilities as capabilities ("You can develop them further through exercise and practice.").

People who rely on fixed mind-sets often adopt victim mentalities: Things happen to them that they simply can't control. But people who adopt growth mentalities see themselves as in control of their own destinies. Although bad circumstances may arise, those with growth mentalities look for ways to flourish even when they are severely challenged. Just as a boat can tack into the wind or an investor can short a stock in a bear market, people with growth mind-sets can move forward and profit despite the forces working against them.

For academic leaders, this growth mind-set might be demonstrated by focusing on the opportunities for personal or professional growth during stressful times. They ask themselves the following questions:

- What skills could I develop or improve by handling this situation?
- How could I use my success in dealing with this problem as evidence that I'm effective as an academic leader and thus advance my career?
- Which benefits, to myself or others, will emerge from this situation?
- What resources do I have available to help me overcome these difficulties? In other words, in what ways am I a resourceful academic leader?

FINAL THOUGHTS ABOUT EMBRACING STRESS

The degree to which eustress and the other aspects of embracing stress are effective for you may depend on your stress threshold, as indicated on the Excitement Tolerance Inventory that you completed in chapter 12. If your score on that inventory was high, you deal well with situations that are suspenseful or thrilling, and so techniques that seek to transform stress into excitement play to your strengths. If you had a low score on the Excitement Tolerance Inventory, however, you tend not to enjoy pastimes that produce a great deal of excitement. For that reason, changing stress into excitement doesn't work very well for you. You'd merely be exchanging one thing that makes you uncomfortable for another.

Fortunately, Selye's concept of eustress and the other ways of embracing stress that we've considered constitute only one of four major approaches to dealing with stress. So, if the techniques explored in this chapter don't seem as though they would help you very much, don't worry. We'll turn next to a technique that is often far more effective for people with a low tolerance for excitement: *stress reduction*.

Chapter 14

Reducing Stress

The second major strategy that we'll consider, *reducing stress*, consists of *identifying as many situations as possible that trigger your stress and then avoiding the triggers when possible or dealing with them more skillfully when you can't simply avoid them*. On the Personal Stress Inventory that you completed at the end of chapter 12, you drew up a list of *predisposing triggers* (the sorts of things that cause your tension to build up over time) and a list of *precipitating triggers* (the sorts of things that "push you over the edge" or cause your stress level to spike immediately).

As a first approach toward reducing stress, we're going to further subdivide each of those two lists into two categories: triggers over which you have at least some control and those over which you have very little or no control. For example, let's suppose that one of your predisposing triggers is being in crowds. You notice that whenever lots of other people are around, you begin to feel under pressure. The high level of background noise when many others are talking makes it difficult for you to focus on what any one person is saying, and you can feel yourself becoming increasingly anxious, uncomfortable, and distracted.

You have at least some control over this trigger. Although being with many other people will occur inevitably in certain work situations, there are plenty of other times when you can decide to avoid crowds. You can shop online instead of dealing with the throngs of people who head to the mall at holiday time. You can plan your commute to and from work so that you travel when there are fewer cars on the road. You can go to meals at times when restaurants aren't as busy, and so on. In short, you've got options. You can control the amount of exposure you have to this trigger at least some of the time.

On the other hand, let's suppose that one of your triggers is meeting with your boss. For whatever reason, every time you're in a room with your

Table 14.1 Four Types of Triggers

	Predisposing Triggers	Precipitating Triggers
Controllable	Predisposing triggers over which you have at least some control	Precipitating triggers over which you have at least some control
Uncontrollable	Predisposing triggers you can't control	Precipitating triggers you can't control

supervisor, your tension increases, and you sometimes feel as though you're on the verge of panic. This situation is very different from that which a person for whom being in crowds is a trigger for stress might face. You can't very easily avoid your boss, and you probably don't even have that much control over when and where your boss wants to meet with you.

Since the techniques for reducing stress are different for controllable and uncontrollable triggers, divide your lists of predisposing and precipitating triggers into two parts so that you end up with four different categories as shown in Table 14.1.

Be sure to complete these lists before you continue since we'll use different strategies to reduce stress in each of these four categories.

PREDISPOSING TRIGGERS YOU CAN CONTROL

When you are dealing with predisposing triggers that you can control, your most effective strategy is often to *desensitize yourself to them*. Since you're able, at least to some degree, to determine when and how you're exposed to these triggers, use that capacity to structure that exposure in such a way that you'll diminish the effect the trigger has on you over time. Your response to a predisposing trigger has been conditioned over time. So, what you'll need to do is to develop a new stimulus/response pattern in which your response is not stress or anxiety but something more productive. That's done in the following way:

Step One. Choose a time and environment in which you're as relaxed as possible. If you need to induce greater relaxation, use one or more of the methods that we'll explore in chapter 15.
Step Two. Expose yourself mentally to the trigger. To put it simply, just think about the trigger for a minute or two. Then return to thinking more pleasant or relaxing thoughts. Once again, use the stress management

techniques from chapter 15 if necessary. Remain on this step for at least two weeks.

Step Three. Increase your mental exposure. To the degree that you find it tolerable, increase the time you spend exposing yourself mentally to your predisposing trigger. Progress from a minute or two to five or six minutes to ten or fifteen minutes. When necessary, return to thinking pleasant thoughts or using your preferred stress management techniques. Continue with this process for at least two weeks or longer if you find that you're not able to think about the trigger for at least fifteen minutes without entering a state of noticeable stress or anxiety.

Step Four. Move from mental images of the trigger to actual experience of the trigger. Use your ability to control your exposure to the trigger to ramp up the degree to which you experience it gradually over time. For instance, if the trigger is a particular place (such as a conference room where tense meetings regularly occur), go there when very few people are around. Initially you may just go to the place, consciously note that you're there, and then leave immediately. Just as you did with the mental exercise, lengthen this exposure gradually over time. If the trigger is a person, seek out a brief contact that is as routine and nonthreatening as possible. Gradually expand your interactions through short conversations and then longer discussions. As always, revert to soothing thoughts or stress management techniques when you need to. This step may take anywhere from three weeks to a full year, depending on the severity of your stress reaction.

Step Five. Reflect on what occurs during an actual or unplanned exposure to the trigger. Once you've done what you can to "build up immunity" to the trigger, see if you find that your response to the stimulus is different in situations that are *not* of your own choosing. If you discover that your stress levels are still increasing whenever you're exposed to this trigger, return to Step Two and repeat the process until you reach the level of desensitization that you need.

PRECIPITATING TRIGGERS YOU CAN CONTROL

Unlike predisposing triggers, precipitating triggers by their very nature tend to cause us to have an intense, immediate reaction. In fact, it's the intensity and immediacy of that reaction that causes us to "go over the edge" when a number of predisposing triggers set the stage for our anxiety or stress. For this reason, even though the process of desensitization that we used for predisposing triggers may eventually reduce their impact on us, it's not an effective strategy for most people. Even thinking about the trigger makes them too stressed out to continue, and small exposures to the actual trigger may prove to be counterproductive.

As a result, the best way to deal with precipitating triggers you can control is to *avoid them*. In other words, since you don't *have* to encounter these triggers, at least on a regular basis, take whatever steps you can to minimize your exposure to these triggers, and don't subject yourself to them. Earlier in this chapter, we considered the case of a person whose stress level increased whenever he or she was in crowds. That person can do more shopping online so as to avoid holiday crowds at the mall and change the time when he or she commutes so as to avoid rush hour traffic. That's not merely running away from a problem; it's recognizing that being exposed to a certain type of situation isn't helpful and making a conscious decision to decrease one's exposure.

How might this strategy work in an academic leadership situation? Let's suppose you have a colleague who, for whatever reason, "pushes your buttons." Perhaps you've tried having a conversation—or a series of conversations—with this person in an attempt to change his or her behavior but without success.

Since you've included this person in the category of precipitating triggers that you can control, your best choice is simply to take control! Choose a different seat in meetings so that this person is neither beside you nor in your line of vision. Change your route to and from other offices so as to make it less likely that you'll cross paths. If the person asks you to go to lunch or for a coffee, mention that you have another commitment. If the person shows up at social events, immerse yourself in conversations with others.

In general, your approach when dealing with triggers over which you have at least some control is to shift from a reactive strategy (where you respond only when your stress is already increased) to a proactive strategy (where you use the control that you have to your own advantage). In this way, you're taking an important step toward shifting from *stress management* to *stress leadership*.

PREDISPOSING TRIGGERS YOU CANNOT CONTROL

Of course, the factors that usually concern us the most are not the ones we can control but those that we feel are completely or largely beyond our control. It's one thing to avoid an irritating colleague. But as we've seen, you can't really avoid an irritating boss. So, how do you deal with those triggers when it's impossible for you to avoid or become immune to them?

The first part of the technique we'll explore is known in cognitive behavioral therapy as *making the covert overt*. In other words, we'll try to make you think more consciously about some of the factors that subconsciously cause you stress. Triggers are often threatening to us, not because they themselves are dangerous, but because we connected them with things that we regard as sources of danger.

In many cases, we may not even be aware of that association. So, before we can "defuse the trigger," we first have to discover what that trigger is connected to.

Let's take the example of a dean who finds that one of his or her predisposing triggers is attending the provost's weekly meetings with the other deans. What is it about those meetings that serve to feed the dean's stress and anxiety? There are many possibilities:

- Any sort of meeting may increase the dean's level of stress if he or she is a very private person who simply feels uncomfortable in group settings.
- The location where the meeting takes place may have been the site of an unpleasant event that still evokes bad memories.
- The dean may be afraid of seeming unprepared or less confident in front of his or her colleague.
- One particular person in attendance may provoke stress in the dean, perhaps because that person is a bully, frequently disparages the dean in public, or engages in other behavior that causes the dean anxiety.
- The dean may be afraid of the provost, either because he or she is generally intimidated by authority figures or because of the provost's interpersonal style.

Plenty of other possibilities also exist. The point is that it's almost impossible to begin dealing with this predisposing trigger unless you know what danger you actually perceive. After all, the solution you might seek if the room itself makes you uncomfortable will be quite different from what you might do if the provost happens to remind you of a previous boss who was difficult to work with.

It's not easy to ask yourself to assess precisely what it is you're afraid of and to acknowledge it as candidly as possible, but that's an important part of dealing with predisposing stress triggers we can't control. So, think very carefully until you can identify precisely what it is—your job, your personal safety, your livelihood, your self-esteem—that you believe to be in jeopardy when you're exposed to these triggers. Then, once you've made this covert concern overt, you can proceed to the second part of this technique: *cognitive restructuring*.

Cognitive restructuring is basically reframing the way in which you think about what you've been regarding as a threat. As we saw in chapter 12, stress is your body's response to a *perceived* threat. But not every threat that we perceive is real. As Mark Twain once said, "Some of the worst things in my life never even happened." It's just that we become so worried that they *might* happen that we start to believe they're *likely* to happen.

If we think about the situation more logically, however, we realize how remote and unlikely the threat actually is. And we're able to think about that threat more logically now that we've made ourselves consciously aware of what we're really afraid of.

Here are a few examples of how this type of cognitive restructuring might work. Suppose you realize that what you're really concerned about when you go into a meeting with the provost and other deans is the possibility that you'll look unprepared or incompetent in front of your boss and peers. Cognitive restructuring would then include asking yourself questions like the following:

- Have I ever actually been blindsided in the way that I'm feeling stressed about? If so, is there something unusual about that situation that makes a similar occurrence unlikely? Or did I learn my lesson well enough that I now prepare adequately? If not, am I being irrational in my concerns? Am I perhaps feeling nothing more than a common desire to be seen as good at what I do, a feeling that probably everyone else in the room (including the provost) shares?
- Is it possible to reduce my concerns by being proactive, perhaps by requesting to receive the meeting agenda in advance so that I can better prepare for the topics that are about to be discussed?
- Could I have access to information I might need at the meeting, perhaps through a Wi-Fi-capable tablet that would give me the confidence that, if specific information is needed, I have a way of obtaining it?

Or suppose your stress increases at these meetings because one of your colleagues tends to act like a bully in them. You might reduce your stress in this area by considering all the resources you have at your disposal like an Employee Assistance Plan that might include training sessions on how to deal with bullies in the workplace, professionals in the Human Resources Office who can advise you on how best to handle these situations, a candid conversation with the provost who may be unaware of how one of his or her deans is treating other members of the group, and so on.

At its core, predisposing triggers of stress tend to affect us for one or both of the following reasons:

- There is a disconnect between what our experience is and what we believe it should be. In this case, we may need to realign our expectations.
- There is a disconnect between what we perceive our resources to be and what we perceive the demands of the situation to be. In this case, we may need to reevaluate our understanding of our resources.

If the first two parts of this technique (making the covert overt and cognitive restructuring) aren't enough to enable you to deal more effectively with the predisposing trigger, the third element of the technique comes into play: *reaching out for a life preserver*. A life preserver is some person, idea, or object that you can reach out to mentally at difficult moments and use to help you cope with the stress of the predisposing trigger.

People who become stressed while giving formal speeches use mental life preservers all the time, even though they may not be consciously aware that they're doing so. The familiar recommendation to imagine the members of your audience naked as you give a speech is supposed to make you feel less intimidated in a setting that many people find challenging.

While that technique doesn't work very well for many people—it can actually increase their stress level and make them feel even more self-conscious—it's based on a useful strategy: leveling the playing field somehow and allowing the speaker to feel less apprehensive. It is, in short, a life preserver.

A more practical life preserver used by many public speakers is to identify one or two friendly faces in the crowd. Even the most hostile audience usually contains at least a handful of people who smile (or simply don't scowl) as you speak and may occasionally nod their heads, indicating that they're following your argument, although they may not yet fully agree with you.

Speakers use these audience members as life preservers during difficult speeches, mentally addressing their remarks to them and transforming in their minds a formal speech into an intimate conversation. They then find that they can relax by knowing that, no matter what the reaction of others may be, they've at least communicated their message effectively to these kind faces in the crowd.

You can find that type of life preserver in other situations as well. Earlier we considered the example of the dean who felt stressed in a meeting of the provost's council. In a situation like that, an occasional glance at another dean whose demeanor seems kind and supportive can provide a kind of life preserver. In other situations, people sometimes use the motto, "This, too, shall pass," as a life preserver to remind themselves that easier times are likely yet to come. In truly severe situations, a life preserver can even be a thought like, "only two more years until my term as chair ends," or, "only five more years until retirement."

A life preserver is thus often a device that's either very personal to you or grounded in the specific situation that is causing you stress. It allows you to cope with the pressure of the situation long enough to get through the current challenge and avoid the risk of a predisposing trigger escalating into a precipitating one.

PRECIPITATING TRIGGERS YOU CANNOT CONTROL

Perhaps the most problematic of all the stress triggers we have are precipitating triggers we can't control. These people, incidents, or places are sufficiently disturbing that they cause an immediate, undesirable reaction in us, and we feel that there's little we can do to prevent them.

Fortunately, if you engage in the stress reduction techniques we've considered for the other triggers, you'll be less likely to have built up a degree of tension and anxiety that leads to the worst results when one of these uncontrollable triggers arises. In addition, there's one helpful strategy you can use in an effort to "disarm" this type of trigger when it does occur.

The strategy is to *adopt a mental model*, and it works in the following way. First, in order to be prepared to deal with precipitating triggers you can't control, you need to be aware of them. So, once again, you want to make the covert overt: Reflect as candidly and objectively as possible on what sorts of things occasion your most intense moments of stress *and why*. As we did before, you need to ask yourself what it is that you're ultimately afraid of and recognize why that particular outcome causes you to become so tensed.

Then, try to identify someone who would respond differently when confronted by such a trigger. This person will be your *mental model*. The person you choose may be actual (Mahatma Gandhi, Mother Teresa, Nelson Mandela, Eleanor Roosevelt) or fictitious (Obi Wan-Kenobi, Katniss Everdeen, Sherlock Holmes, Hermione Granger), as long as you can imagine this person responding appropriately to a stimulus that you yourself might respond to inappropriately or unskillfully. Then, when a precipitating trigger you can't control arises, you momentarily assume the identity of your mental model and ask yourself what that person would do in this situation.

In most cases, adopting a mental model will supply you with a more constructive response than you would ordinarily have given. But even if you decide that your mental model's reaction would not be helpful, pulling back from the troubling situation even for a fraction of a second and viewing it through the eyes of someone else can provide you with a larger perspective and reduce the negative impact the stimulus might have on you.

FINAL THOUGHTS ABOUT REDUCING STRESS

Situations and events that cause us stress often make us feel powerless. We're reduced to a passive state, or so it seems: Something happens, our stress trigger is pulled, and so we respond in ways we feel we can't control. The strategy of stress reduction encourages us to seize control back again in those situations where we haven't felt in control. By using such techniques as desensitizing ourselves to the trigger and restructuring the way we think about threats, we restore ourselves to a position of being in charge of our reactions and mood. Nevertheless, there will still be times when, despite our best efforts, stress gets the better of us. When these situations occur, it's time to resort to the next device we have in our toolkit for coping with stress: stress management.

Chapter 15

Managing Stress

Of all the approaches to dealing with stress that we'll consider, stress management is by far the most common. In fact, it's such a common approach that many workshops and books (including this one) use *stress management* as a shorthand way to refer to everything that has to do with handling stress.

But, as we've seen, managing stress is only one of several ways in which academic leaders can deal with the pressures of the job. Even if you find your ability to handle stress much improved by the strategies we've already considered, you still need to know about ways to manage stress. That's because there will be times when, despite your best efforts, workday stress simply sneaks up on you.

Stress management is an approach that seeks to relieve stress that is already present. In other words, if embracing stress is about *transforming* stress into excitement and reducing stress is about *avoiding* stress as much as possible, managing stress deals with the following question: "The stress is already here. Now what?" The fundamental technique involved in stress management is to identify practices that work *for you* to lower your current level stress and then systematically to engage in those practices during times when you're feeling under pressure.

Since the practices that help us eliminate and control stress are very personal, what works for me may not be the same thing that works for you. For this reason, we have to explore a wide range of stress management techniques so that you can identify the two or three that consistently produce the results you want. The stress management techniques that we'll explore in this chapter are

- deep breathing techniques,
- meditation,

- massage,
- stretching exercises,
- yoga,
- prayer,
- gratitude exercises,
- listening to calming music, and
- spending time in calming environments

With this framework in mind, let's consider each of these practices in turn.

DEEP BREATHING TECHNIQUES

For years, a common belief (at that time unsupported by evidence) was that, if you were stressed about something, you should take a deep breath to calm down. In fact, if you're prone to stress, you've probably had someone tell you, "Just breathe!" on more than one occasion.

But more recent research has demonstrated that this common belief actually has a sound scientific basis. A group of researchers at the Stanford University School of Medicine discovered that a cluster of neurons in the brainstem, known as the pre-Bötzinger complex, functions essentially as a "breath pacemaker"—at least in mice. As a mouse becomes calmer, the pre-Bötzinger complex slows its breathing, and as the mouse becomes more excited, the cluster speeds up its breathing (Yackle, Schwarz, Kam, Sorokin, Huguenard, Feldman, Luo, and Krasnow, 2017).

That discovery alone is an interesting insight, but what makes this research useful for stress management is that *the process also works in reverse*. In other words, slowing the breath *induces calm*, and speeding up the breath *induces excitement*. Based on this information, it's thus possible to establish a pattern of deep breathing that works for many people to control the amount of stress they're under within a relatively brief period of time.

Here's a simple deep breathing technique that you can use almost anywhere:

1. Find a comfortable position.
2. Relax your gaze, or, if you prefer, gently close your eyes; don't squeeze them shut.
3. Establish an intention to relax. Doing so can be as simple as thinking, "I'm going to relax now," or, "This deep breathing exercise will help me relax."
4. Inhale deeply while mentally counting slowly to five. Try to fill your lungs with air as completely as possible.
5. Pause a moment.
6. Exhale while mentally counting slowly to eight. Try to empty your lungs of air as completely as possible. Note that you'll have to exhale more

slowly than you inhaled; otherwise, you'll run out of air before you reach the end of your count.
7. Pause a moment.
8. Return to Step 4, and repeat.

If you continue this technique for at least five minutes, you'll have successfully slowed your breathing and alerted your pre-Bötzinger complex that you've become calmer. That, in turn, will cause messages to be sent to other parts of your nervous system, and you'll end up actually feeling calmer.

Like so much in the modern world, "there's an app for that." For your laptop or desktop computer, the software application Pranayama is highly customizable, allowing you to set a length of time for your inhalation and exhalation that is most comfortable for you. It also provides gentle sound cues, so that you don't have to watch the screen in order to know what to do next. Breathing Zone—Relaxing Breathing Exercises is a bit simpler in design but also customizable, and it provides spoken cues ("Breathe in" and "Breathe out") that some users may find preferable.

Both Pranayama and Breathing Zone—Relaxing Breathing Exercises also exist as apps for cellphones and tablets. But there are also a host of other portable apps, many of them free, that also work on these devices. Breathe+ Relaxation and Breath Training guides your breathing at the same time that it helps you visualize the deep breathing process. Breathe2Relax provides general information about stress management in addition to its deep breathing tool. And Hear and Now: Breathe for Stress and Anxiety Reduction seeks to incorporate your heart rate into a deep breathing exercise to help you better determine your progress.

Of course, you don't really need an app to engage in deep breathing. One of the great advantages of this technique is that it's possible to perform it almost anywhere. If you're not too obvious about what you're doing, you can even practice a little deep breathing in those tense meetings with your boss that usually cause your stress level to rise. Deep breathing techniques are particularly popular stress management approaches because they require no equipment, are easy to learn, and may be performed under a very broad range of conditions.

MEDITATION

Meditation is a technique that, in some of its forms, is so similar to deep breathing that many people confuse the two methods. But meditation is an even more flexible stress management technique that has its own history and that works for some people who don't find deep breathing helpful. (It should be noted that the reverse is true, too: You may discover that deep breathing is effective in managing your stress but meditation is boring or unproductive.) Although meditation and the related concept of mindfulness have received a great deal of attention, there remain many false impressions about what meditation is.

- *Meditation is not (necessarily) a religious activity.* Although certain religious traditions include meditation among their practices, it's also possible to practice meditation simply as a relaxation technique similar to deep breathing. You don't have to adopt any particular set of beliefs in order to do so.
- *Meditation does not involve going into a trance.* When you meditate, you'll be completely aware of what's going on around you. In fact, since the goal of meditation is to increase your mindfulness of experience as it occurs, you'll probably be *more* aware than you usually are of what's happening in your immediate environment.
- *Meditation is not about emptying your mind of all thoughts.* It's about resting your awareness on experience and becoming less distracted over time by disruptive thoughts. But no matter how hard you try, you can't empty your mind of all thoughts for more than a very short time. Thinking thoughts is what minds do naturally.
- *Meditation does not require hard concentration.* When you meditate, you *rest* your awareness on your experience; you don't forcefully direct it toward your experience. That would defeat the whole purpose.

Various schools of meditation have arisen that direct the practitioner's awareness of current experience in different ways. There are far too many schools of meditation to list them all, but the most common approaches are these:

- *Shamatha* or *Anapana Meditation*: awareness of the breath.
- *Vipassana Meditation*: awareness of sensations (often performed by slowly conducting a body scan).
- *Mantra Meditation*: awareness of a specific sound.
- *Metta Meditation*: awareness of compassion or loving-kindness.

Another approach is Tantra Meditation, a more advanced technique that varies greatly depending upon the goal of the teacher and need of the student and that is much more difficult to perform in a secular manner than the other aforementioned techniques.

For our purposes, we will consider merely Shamatha or Anapana Meditation because it's the easiest approach to learn and because all other approaches rely on it as a foundation. In order to practice this form of meditation, you simply do the following:

1. Find a comfortable but alert position. Many people meditate while resting on cushions, but no particular equipment is necessary. You can meditate while sitting in a chair, kneeling, or standing if you prefer. You simply want to find a position where you'll be comfortable without moving—but not so comfortable that you fall asleep—for the duration of the meditation.
2. Rest your hands in a position where you won't be tempted to move them. Some people rest their hands loosely in their laps, others place them palm downwards on their upper legs or knees, and still others let them hang loosely at their sides.
3. Either loosely close your eyes or leave them open but with your eyelids and gaze relaxed. An example of the posture you will then have adopted appears in Figure 15.1.
4. Set a timer for the length of the meditation session you want. If you've never meditated before, underestimate the amount of time you'll want to devote to this practice. Three to five minutes is sufficient for an initial session. Until you become completely familiar with the technique, that time will probably seem very long to you.

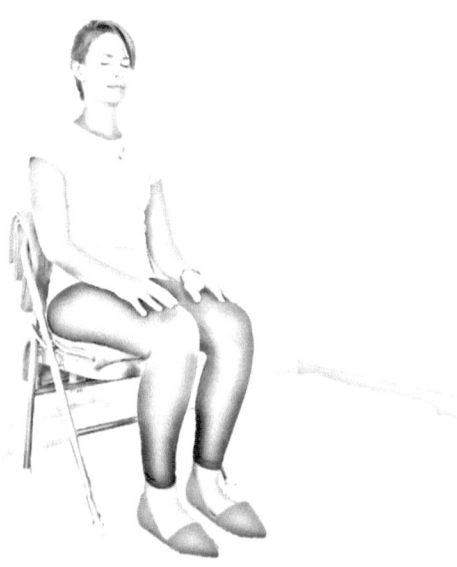

Figure 15.1

5. Slowly take three deep breaths, paying full attention to every sensation you have while inhaling and exhaling.
6. After exhaling the third breath, return to breathing normally.
7. On each subsequent in-breath, let your attention rest on the fact that you're inhaling.
8. On each subsequent out-breath, let your thoughts go where they may.
9. From time to time, you'll notice that your thoughts have continued to stray and that you weren't aware of several in-breaths. That's okay. It's merely part of the exercise. Simply guide your awareness back toward your breath as you inhale and continue meditating.
10. Continue this process until the timer goes off.

That's it! There's nothing more difficult or mysterious about meditation than that.

Like deep breathing, some people find it very relaxing after even their first attempt. Most people, however, have to practice meditation daily for about a month before they begin to notice their stress levels decreasing because of this exercise. (That's another reason to keep your initial sessions short: It's easy to find a spare three to five minutes each day but easy to give up when you're trying to block out twenty or thirty minutes for an activity you're not yet sure is right for you.)

What you may observe is that, even before you yourself feel calmer because of a regular meditation practice, people who know you well start remarking that you seem less stressed than you were before. That's a good indication that your meditation practice is working.

Like deep breathing, some people find that meditation doesn't help them at all, even though they engage in it faithfully for several months. That's why finding the right stress management technique for you may take some experimentation. If you've made a serious effort at deep breathing and meditation and discover that they don't suit your needs, one of the following techniques may be more appropriate for you.

MASSAGE

One activity that most people find relaxing is receiving a massage. The type of massage you find most suitable when you're undergoing a great deal of stress may be quite different from what someone else regards as soothing.

You may enjoy a gentle Swedish massage that is almost like a back rub, calming you and perhaps even lulling you to sleep. Someone else might prefer a more intense, deep tissue massage that feels as though it's ironing the kinks out of his or her tense muscles. And even the amount of pressure people prefer during a massage varies a great deal. Firm, medium, gentle—it's all a matter of individual taste. And some people don't like massage at all; being touched by someone strikes them as a violation of their personal space.

Nevertheless, for people who do enjoy receiving a massage, there are few experiences that can carry them almost instantaneously from a condition of stress and anxiety to one of calm and relaxation. And massage has a number of health benefits as well:

- When we're under pressure, we tend to tighten our muscles, even though we may not be aware of doing so. Prolonged tension of this sort can cause these muscles to become sore and produce a vicious cycle of stress causing tension and tension causing additional stress. Muscle fibers might even tighten to the point that they can't be released even after our stress triggers go away. During massage, our muscles relax and receive a temporary break from the near constant tension our work may expose us to.
- Massage often improves a person's ability to sleep. Lack of sleep leads to a number of problematic health conditions and intensifies our stress level, particularly if we spend most of the night worrying about our problems instead of sleeping. By causing our muscles to fall into the more relaxed position they have during natural sleep, massage often enables people to sleep more deeply than they ordinarily would. Most important of all, these deep sleep states are achieved without medication.
- Massage can reduce some of the discomfort associated with work in a modern office, such as repetitive motion or nerve pressure strains (such as carpal tunnel syndrome) and the discomfort of sitting for long periods. These discomforts often reduce job satisfaction, and job dissatisfaction may lead to depression, increased stress, or both.

Additionally, just the contact with another person that comes about through massage may have health benefits of its own. Certainly, the lack of contact with others—social and physical isolation—has been shown to lead to increased likelihood of dementia in the elderly. It's not impossible that some of those detrimental effects could be avoided by regular touch and interaction with others through practices like massage.

As a stress management technique, it's also possible to combine massage with deep breathing techniques or meditation. Breathing deeply throughout a massage speeds up the process of muscular relaxation. And people who find it tedious to rest their awareness on the breath during traditional meditation often find it quite easy and pleasant to rest their attention on the point of contact the masseuse has with their skin. Although they may not think of it in that way, they're actually engaging in a form of meditation when they do so.

STRETCHING EXERCISES

Because we tend to tighten our muscles when we're tense, many people believe the mere act of stretching those muscles to loosen them serves as a convenient, low-cost means of stress management. The precise muscles you stretch depend on where you notice the greatest tension forming during times of increased pressure. In many cases, it's the muscles of the shoulders and neck that tend to be affected first. For this reason, *neck rolls and stretches* are often the best place to begin when you notice that you're tense.

To perform a neck roll,

1. Start by facing straight ahead with your neck erect and your back straight.
2. Tilt your head to one side, making sure not to move beyond your point of comfort. Stretching is one activity in which the adage "No pain, no gain" definitely does *not* apply.
3. Gradually roll your head from your side to your back until you're looking up toward the ceiling or sky.
4. Continue rolling your head until it's on the opposite side from where you began.
5. Bring your head to the front, rotating it down so that you're now looking at the ground or floor.
6. Rotate your head back upward toward the sky while moving it to the side of your body where you started.
7. Repeat Steps 3 through 6 until you begin to feel your neck and shoulder muscles loosen.
8. End the neck roll by returning your head to the position in Step 1.
9. See Figure 15.2 for an illustration of this process.

You can then follow these neck rolls with one or more of the following neck stretches:

- From the position of your head in Steps 1 and 8, *tilt* your neck slowly, first to your left and then to your right.
- From the position of your head in Steps 1 and 8, *rotate* your neck slowly, first to your left and then to your right.
- Extend both arms behind your back, using each hand to grasp the wrist of your opposite arm. With your right hand, gently pull your left arm, first to the right side of your body and then further away from your back so that your arms are no longer touching your body. Then do the same thing with your left hand, gently pulling your right arm first to the left side of your body and then slightly away from your back.

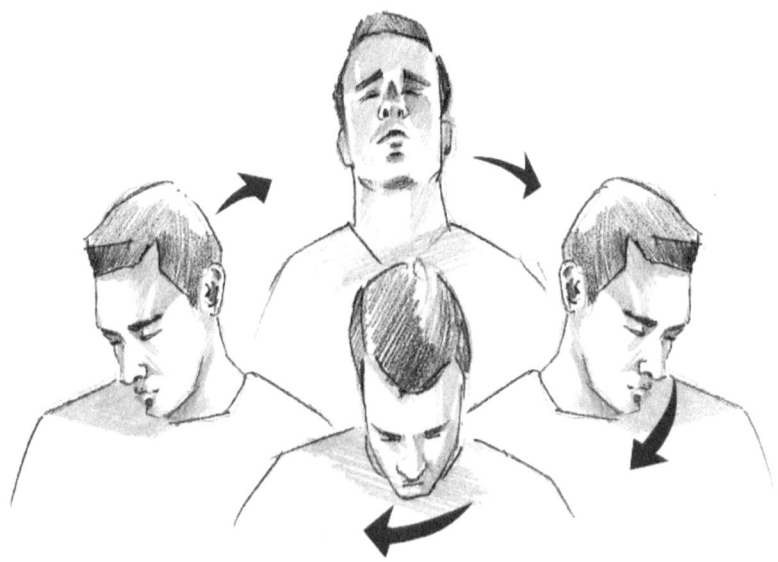

Figure 15.2

If your neck isn't where you feel most tension build, you can use stretching to relax other muscles as well. For example, leg and calf muscles can be safely stretched by starting in a standing position with one foot facing straight forward and your other foot slightly behind it and at a right angle to it, with your toes facing outward. Take a step forward with your front leg, and then bend it at the knee, holding your rear leg straight. Repeat this bend five or six times. Then reverse the positions of your feet, and do the same thing with your other leg.

As with all stretching exercises, don't continue to the point of causing yourself any pain. Merely bend far enough so that you can feel a slight, comfortable pull on the muscles of your straight leg.

Trained massage therapists are also experienced with how best to stretch your muscles. In addition to a regular massage, you might consider asking the masseuse to guide you in stretching any muscles where you feel particularly tense because of the stress you experience as an academic leader.

YOGA

A more formal and systematic approach to stretching can be found in the variety of activities that are referred to collectively in the West as yoga. In the East, yoga first developed as a religious practice and was often seen as a method that could be used for attaining enlightenment. In the West, these religious dimensions of yoga tend to be given less significance, and emphasis is placed on physical types of yoga, such as *hatha yoga* (which emphasizes posture and breathing styles) and *bikram yoga* (in which postures are adopted in a heated space), as opposed to other forms that emphasize contemplation, sacrifice, and other spiritual activities.

Although many people assume that yoga is largely a type of stretching exercise, yoga as it's practiced in the West has two primary differences from the types of stretching we just explored. First, yoga usually integrates breathing and the adoption of certain postures. For this reason, it may be regarded as something of a combination of deep (or at least intentional or conscious) breathing, meditation, and stretching.

Second, yoga poses usually fall into two groups: *active yoga poses*, in which the practitioner is indeed stretching or balancing in order to obtain a certain posture, and *passive yoga poses*, in which the practitioner merely maintains a certain posture, often using a bolster, wall, pillow, or cushion for support.

The following are a few common yoga poses that are typically associated with stress management:

- *The Thunderbolt Pose (Vajrasana)*. Kneel on a mat or thin cushion so that your lower legs are flat behind you. Sit back on your lower legs, which should now be facing downward. (If that position is too uncomfortable, you may slip a cushion or pillow between your legs and buttocks and sit backward on it.) Adopt an erect posture so that your spine is straight upward but not tight or uncomfortable. Gently extend your neck slightly upward as though someone from above were gently lifting your head. Rest your hands, palms facing downward, on your upper thighs. Breathe deeply and attentively ten or twelve times in this posture. See Figure 15.3.
- *The Corpse Pose (Savasana)*. Lie down with your back on a mat or a thin cushion. Rest your arms a short distance from your body at your side, palms upward, so that your entire body, from the back of your head to your heels, is resting on the mat or cushion. You can roll a towel or use a pillow to support your neck if you wish. Gradually proceeding from your feet to your head, make a conscious effort to relax each set of muscles in your body. Once your muscles are relaxed, begin breathing deeply and attentively. Rest in this pose for about five minutes. See Figure 15.4.
- *The Extended Triangle Pose (Trikonasana)*. Stand with your legs to your sides about four feet apart from one another. Turn your right foot out so that it is facing to the side. Place your right hand on your right leg and slide it down toward your foot as far as you can. Extend your left arm upward so that your right and left arms form a single line, and look upward toward your left hand. When you reach the point beyond which it is uncomfortable

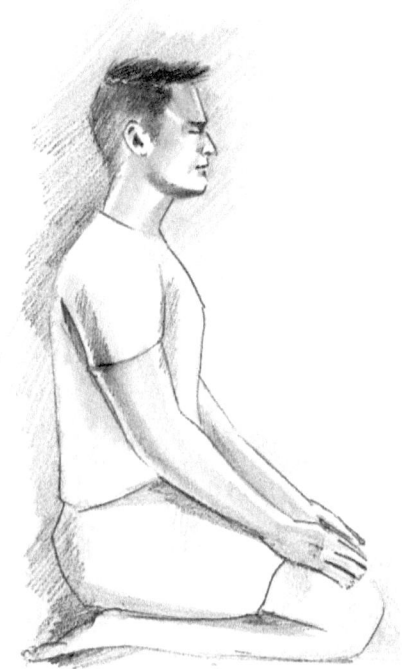

Figure 15.3

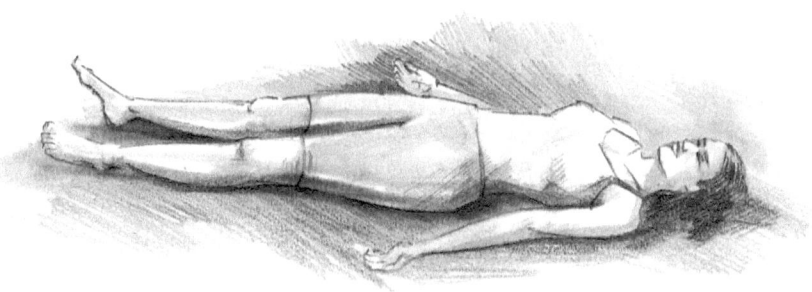

Figure 15.4

Figure 15.5

to stretch, hold this posture for a minute or two. As you maintain this position, breathe deeply and attentively. Then reverse legs and perform the same kind of bend to your left side. Repeat this alternation of stretches and breathing three to five times. See Figure 15.5.

There are many more poses that can be used for stress relief, and, if you find this approach useful, your best option is to explore a few additional postures by means of YouTube videos or DVDs and then, if you are truly serious, join a formal yoga class. Most centers offering classes provide instruction at various levels, so inquire about a beginner's or restorative yoga class before attempting poses that may be too difficult for you. Also be aware that different teachers often have their own preferences about exactly how each move is performed, so don't be surprised if your teacher describes the poses mentioned earlier somewhat differently from how they're presented here.

PRAYER

Many people find that faith and spirituality are important aspects of their lives. Through faith and spirituality, they feel they have a sense of meaning and purpose, become grounded in what's important, and see "the big picture" rather than the stresses of the moment. By praying, they unburden themselves of their troubles and are reminded of a higher power in the universe that they believe can help guide them through their troubles.

Prayer that becomes merely a litany of whatever is stressing the person can, however, be counterproductive. Rather than releasing themselves from the pressures they are under, people who pray only to recite their sufferings often keep their wounds fresh and find themselves even less able to put stress behind them than they were before they prayed. For this reason, one structure for prayer that some people find useful is the following:

1. *Request*. Recognize that you're experiencing a situation that has put you under a great deal of stress that you feel unable to handle by yourself. Ask for assistance in dealing with the anxiety and tension that this situation has produced.
2. *Thanksgiving*. Express gratitude for the good things that are indeed still occurring in your life and the world. Be thankful for past favors and acknowledge the role that your faith has played in bringing those good things into your life.
3. *Confidence*. Conclude your prayer by making a firm resolution that, based on past grace that has been received and the strength of your faith, you know that you will receive the help you need to get through the stress you're currently under. In the words of the common maxim, "Let go and let God."

Of course, not everyone has an active faith in God. In the West at least, surveys repeatedly demonstrate an inverse relationship between the amount of formal education people have and their belief in God. Since academic leaders are, as a group, people who have a high level of formal education, we can expect that they will generally be more skeptical about matters of religion than the general population. So, is there any role for prayer for a nonbeliever? Can people who don't believe in spirits be spiritual? Or, to put the matter bluntly, can you have a mental conversation with someone you don't believe exists?

One activity that bears some similarities to prayer but that does not require a belief in God is a practice associated with the metta approach to mindfulness. We've already encountered the term *metta* in connection with one of four major types of meditation. It is a word found in Pali (a language related to Sanskrit) that means something like *benevolence* or *loving-kindness*. With metta mindfulness, you begin by identifying three people:

1. Someone you like.
2. Someone you're indifferent to.
3. Someone you dislike.

And then you add to this list:

4. Yourself.
5. Everyone in the world.

The practice of metta mindfulness then consists of going through this list in sequence, thinking the following thoughts about each person or group: "May he/she/I/they be happy. May he/she/I/they be healthy. May he/she/I/they be safe. May he/she/I/they be free from care."

For example, let's suppose that the person you care deeply about is named Jamie, the person you're indifferent to is your bookstore manager (whom you don't even know well enough to be familiar with his or her name), and the person you dislike is named Landry. Your mindfulness exercise will consist of thinking the following thoughts in this sequence:

- May Jamie be happy. May Jamie be healthy. May Jamie be safe. May Jamie be free from care.
- May our bookstore manager be happy. May our bookstore manager be healthy. May our bookstore manager be safe. May our bookstore manager be free from care.
- May Landry be happy. May Landry be healthy. May Landry be safe. May Landry be free from care.
- May I be happy. May I be healthy. May I be safe. May I be free from care.
- May everyone in the world be happy. May everyone in the world be healthy. May everyone in the world be safe. May everyone in the world be free from care.

Once you've completed your list, you can return to the first person and start over, repeating this exercise as long as you like.

If you believe in the power of prayer, you might think of yourself as actually asking a higher power to guide and protect everyone on your list. But the important part of metta mindfulness is that you don't actually have to believe in God or the power of prayer to make this activity useful. When you think a thought like "May so-and-so be happy," you're not necessarily petitioning the universe on this person's behalf. Instead, you can think of this exercise as a way of reminding yourself to be kind and compassionate toward those you like, those you don't like, those you don't know (or at least don't know well), and yourself.

GRATITUDE EXERCISES

That reminder that we ourselves need compassion and understanding no less than others around us should also help us recall that, despite all the pressures we face as academic leaders, we also have people who care about us and many other aspects in our lives for which we should be grateful.

One of the reasons why we feel so stressed is that, due to the pressure of our workload, we're off onto the next challenge the moment we've finished the last challenge. We too infrequently have an opportunity to bask in the glory of our successes, celebrate the things that are going right, or demonstrate gratitude to the other people who made those successes possible.

Engaging in intentional, planned exercises of gratitude thus not only improves morale for us and our coworkers—they feel less taken for granted, and we feel less callous for ignoring them—but also improves our awareness of the present moment. They force us to pause briefly, recognize the achievements that are being made in our areas, and regroup before moving on.

Perhaps the best gratitude exercise you can engage in is a weekly inventory of "five good things." Before you go home at the end of the week or just before you begin work at the start of the week, spend a minute or two listing "five good things that happened in our program this week" or "five good things that my colleagues did last week."

If you perform this exercise more frequently than once a week, it merely becomes a chore, one more item on your to-do list. If you perform it less frequently or more randomly, you're probably not engaging in the exercise often enough for it to have much effect. But a few minutes of gratitude once a week can go a long way toward making your job seem less stressful and your colleagues seem less irritating.

A variation of this exercise is to keep a gratitude journal. Start a note on your cellphone or a blank document on your computer, and, every time something happens that you feel grateful for, jot it down. It only takes a few seconds to make this note, but when you're having one of those particularly stressful days when nothing seems to be going right, you'll have a list you can consult that should make it clear just how much you have to be grateful for in your life and work.

The reason why these exercises work is that expressions of gratitude tend to make us feel less stressed. They remind us that we're not alone, that we have a network of support.

And each of us has his or her own pattern of gratitude. Some people thank others for every small thing they do. Others rarely express gratitude unless someone goes above and beyond the call of duty in a major, almost life-changing manner. And there's every level of expression in between. The key to an effective gratitude exercise is to reflect on what your own pattern of gratitude happens to be and then increase the frequency of it—just slightly.

If you try to go from a person who rarely even acknowledges the staff at a restaurant to thanking them every time they perform even the slightest service, you'll exhaust yourself. The practice will feel artificial, and you'll give up on it quickly. The most effective way to expand your pattern of gratitude is to *thank one more person a day than you would have done otherwise*. In other words, if you find that you naturally say "thank you" to people half a dozen times a day, try doing so seven times. If you do so a 100 times a day, try 101.

It's that extra little conscious effort of gratitude that makes the difference. For that brief moment each day, the exercise takes you a bit outside of your own world of stress and pressures and makes one person feel valued who might not otherwise have had that experience.

Academic leaders who have engaged in this exercise have told me how rapidly it seems to work. If they keep it up for as little as two weeks, they find themselves generally feeling less stressed at work. And if they keep it up for at least a month, some say that it has a noticeable effect on others. Offices that had been highly politicized became less so, and the amount of destructive conflict and tension seemed to have decreased.

LISTENING TO CALMING MUSIC

For most people, music has an effect on mood that's profound and almost immediate. Composers of soundtracks for movies have long used music to set or reinforce the tone of a scene. Rousing, exhilarating music increases our level of excitement. Soft, slow, gentle music produces a feeling of calm.

Sometimes in movies, we're not even aware of the music in the background that is creating the mood we feel as we watch the scene. But if you want evidence of music's power to evoke particular feelings, just search the Internet for the original teaser trailer of the movie *Star Wars* (1977) before John Williams composed his score. Scenes that were thrilling in the final version of the film seem stilted, flat, and even a bit silly.

Of course, the music that each of us finds calming is a very personal matter. One person's taste might lead to Mozart or Brahms, another's to folk ballads, and still another's to ambient or "spa" music. The key is simply to identify the type of music that works for you and to have it readily available on days when you're undergoing a great deal of stress at work.

You may not, of course, be able to play that music aloud if you're in an environment where it disturbs others. You may not even be able to use a headset if your work requires you to be readily able to hear other people's questions. But if you have your music for stress management available, perhaps as a playlist on your phone or tablet, you can make use of it as soon as you can take a moment or two for a break, head to lunch, or walk to the next meeting.

Remember, too, that the music that calms you doesn't have to be literal music. A recording of waves lapping at the shore, gentle breezes wafting through the pines, or babies giggling and murmuring might restore your sense of peace and your belief that "all's right with the world" faster than an actual melody. Calming music, in other words, can include any sounds that you personally find relaxing and that enable you to handle the pressures of your work with a clearer mind.

SPENDING TIME IN CALMING ENVIRONMENTS

Relaxing images and settings function in much the same way that calming music does. They can have an almost instantaneous impact on our moods and cause us to feel refreshed and tranquil without much effort on our part. Like music, however, the environments that each of us finds calming can be very personal. Where one person views the majesty of a mountain scene as a comforting reminder of nature's beauty, others can regard mountains as symbols of obstacles to be overcome and, with their sharp edges and avalanches, of threats that appear when we least expect them.

You probably already know which settings help you unwind. Maybe you like to go to the beach on vacation. Maybe you find yourself becoming calm by a stroll through a garden. A chapel, mosque, or synagogue may make you feel more grounded the moment you pass through its doors. The important thing is to be aware of the settings that work best for you and to identify appropriate places (or reasonable approximations) that are near enough to your home or work for you to escape to when you need to.

A five-minute visit to a calming environment on the way home after a particularly trying day can provide just the release you need to make a smooth transition from your job to your personal life. A ten-minute visit to the campus art gallery over your lunch hour can prevent you from transferring the stresses of the morning to the meetings and appointments of the afternoon. And, if it's absolutely impossible for you to visit these places physically, is there some way that you can visit them "virtually" throughout the workday?

A seascape or forest scene can make a good background image for your computer desktop. A photograph of your favorite place on earth can be placed on your desk, tucked in a drawer for those times when you need to pull it out and just have a moment or two of mental escape, or set as your screen saver so that it greets you every time you're away from your computer for more than a few minutes.

We'll explore further variations on these ideas when we talk about the techniques of the Mental Vacation and the Serene Refuge in chapter 16. However you find it most practical to employ this technique, the key questions are always, "Where would I go to relax if I could go anywhere?" and, "How can I fit in a visit to that place, either in person or virtually, during my day on a regular basis?"

FINAL THOUGHTS ABOUT MANAGING STRESS

Where a lot of efforts at dealing with stress run rampant is in people's efforts to use these stress management techniques in isolation, without considering all the other strategies that we explore in this book. As a result, they have a tense day at work, get a massage, relax while they're actually with the masseuse, but then return to their regular levels of stress as soon as they leave the table.

Stress management is most effective when it's combined with other strategies into a holistic approach to dealing with the pressures of being an academic leader, including pressures on your time. That's the topic we'll consider in chapter 17.

But before we do that, there's one more set of strategic questions about stress we need to answer, and those are, "What do you do when you've tried everything we've discussed so far—you've attempted to embrace, reduce, and manage your stress—and still find yourself unable to deal with the pressures of your job? What do you do then? How do you cope with stress that, for whatever reason, you simply can't embrace, avoid, or manage?" That's the topic that we'll turn to in our next chapter.

Chapter 16

Coping with Stress

There are times when, no matter what we do, we can't find a productive way to deal with the stress of being an academic leader. Despite our best efforts, it can almost seem as though circumstances (and perhaps even people) conspire against us to increase our tension and cause us anxiety. Most of the time, we just try to grit our teeth and bear it. But there are, in fact, more productive techniques we can try when we have no other choice but to cope with it.

THE MENTAL VACATION

The first few coping mechanisms that we'll consider all derive from a single concept: How can you provide yourself with "an out" when actual, physical escape from a stressful environment is simply not possible? One way to apply this concept is to *imagine* yourself in some comforting, relaxing space if you can't actually go there. You choose a *mental vacation spot* by visualizing, in as much realistic detail as possible, the most stress-free, tranquil environment possible.

In the last chapter, you identified an actual environment that you find calming. If you like, you may use that same environment as your mental vacation spot. But you can also use your creativity to imagine the ideal place to go in order to alleviate the pressures of your job. If you have some difficulty fleshing out all the details of what this place might be like, here are a few guiding questions that may assist you.

- In what general setting would you find it easiest to relax? The beach? The desert? At home? A church, chapel, temple, mosque, or synagogue? On a mountain? Driving down an open highway?

- What temperature do you feel on your skin? Is it cool? Warm? Somewhere in between?
- What other sensations do you feel? Do you notice a slight breeze? A gentle rain? Sunlight? Nothing at all?
- What sounds do you hear? The soft splashing of waves? Raindrops? Wildlife? Soft voices? Something else? Nothing?
- What do you smell? Perfume? Fresh air? Seawater? Incense? Nothing at all?
- Are you with people or alone? If one or more other people are there, who has joined you?
- How do your muscles feel?
- What else would you add to this mental image to make it the perfect setting?

In the interest of full disclosure, I should mention that some people speak dismissively of this concept as "going to your happy place." But the fact of the matter is that allowing yourself a mental vacation, even for a few seconds during a tense meeting or conversation, can help you cope better with the stress of the situation. By having our mental vacation spots designed vividly in our own minds, we can "go to" them at a moment's notice whenever we need to. They provide that short break or safe haven for us when no physical alternative is possible.

So, ignore all the naysayers who might mock you if they knew that you "were going to your happy place" the next time you need to cope with stress. This technique is for you, not them, and it can leave you in a far better condition to deal with all the irritations of academic leadership—like those naysayers.

THE SERENE REFUGE

The concept of the Serene Refuge combines the idea of the Mental Vacation with that of the calming environments that we explored in the last section. To create a Serene Refuge, you begin by considering what it is about certain places that make them relaxing for you. It may be that the lighting there is soft and natural as opposed to harsh and artificial. It may be that there are certain colors, sounds, or scents that you find soothing. Or it may be that there are certain people there who always help you to relax. You might want to perform an Internet search on topics like *relaxing images*, *zen office décor*, *serene workplace*, and the like to get some ideas about how those soothing elements of particular environments can be translated into something suitable for the professional environment.

Naturally, if you do that, you'll probably come up with lots of ideas that are absolutely unsuitable for your own workspace. Few of us can afford professional decorators to design our offices and, even if we could, many of us don't have the large, open offices that are commonly depicted in the type of interior design publications that create these images.

The goal isn't to replicate these sometimes luxurious settings, but rather to gather ideas about what makes them appealing. Dark, light, or medium wood tones? Small fountains? A clean, well-lit space or a comforting, cozy space? Then, with that knowledge in hand, try to identify a few specific things that you *can* do—within your budget and in line with your institution's policies— that would make your own workspace more of a serene refuge.

In creating this environment for yourself, you also have to think of other people. That fountain that you find soothing may create a sound that others find distracting. That lavender scent that you find relaxing may intensify the allergic reactions of those around you. So, before you do anything specific, be sure to check with those whom the changes in your personal workspace might affect. It won't be a tranquil environment for you if, every time you go there, you're reminded of how much your innovations bother other people.

Even the smallest change can sometimes make a big difference. Turning off the overhead lighting and using floor and desk lamps instead can utterly transform an office. Clearing away the clutter that you may have collected over the years and making your desk more orderly can have an immediate impact on your frame of mind. A photo of that friend, loved one, or deceased relative who always made you happy in his or her presence can comfort you on a really stressful day.

Even in the worst, most anxiety-filled meetings that you have, you'll find it easier to cope with these difficulties by recalling that you have a Serene Refuge waiting for you when you get back to your workspace.

THE SERENE MOMENT

Often when we're under a great deal of stress, particularly when we're stressed out from all the things on our to-do lists, we feel we have to work harder and faster. We stop taking breaks and extend our workdays into the time when we should be resting or even sleeping. Ironically, those efforts are frequently counterproductive. We experience diminishing returns when we work nonstop. Study after study has indicated that people are far more productive if they work for fifty or fifty-five minutes every hour and take a break for five or ten minutes.

Those breaks can become our Serene Moments. There are times when, as counterintuitive as it may sound, we have to get our minds off of our work in order to become more effective at our work.

To have their greatest impact, Serene Moments should immerse you in some experience that you find relaxing. Using them to catch up on personal e-mails or to update your status on your social media accounts probably won't refresh you very much. Instead, Serene Moments might consist of activities such as the following:

- Think back to your very first day in this position. Do you remember how excited you were (and let's be frank: probably a little nervous, too, although it was eustress or the "good kind" of nervous; see chapter 13)? You probably wore something special, made sure you were well groomed, and felt good about yourself for getting this job. Well, there's good news: *You still have that job!* So, devote a few moments to recalling why you were so happy to have it in the first place.
- Reflect on your achievements and the positive qualities you have that helped you achieve them. Instead of stressing about how much you have to do, give yourself permission to take five or ten minutes and reflect on everything you've already done. Bask in the good memories, even pausing to count your many important contributions that have made other people's lives better. Reflect that, it isn't really that you have so much to do; it's that you're the kind of person who gets so much done.
- Savor your refreshments. If you're taking a coffee break, assign full weight to both of those words: Truly taste the *coffee*, breathing in its aroma and allowing its warmth to relax you; and truly remember that you're on a *break*, not just away from your desk so that you can keep working in a different location. If you don't particularly like coffee, your serene moment can be devoted to any type of snack or beverage you prefer (as long as it is permissible in the workplace). Experience it. Direct all your thoughts toward it for a few minutes. Revel in it.

Those five or ten minutes aren't wasted or distractions from your work. They're necessary restoratives that will make you more effective at your work at the same time that they cause you to become less stressed about it.

STRATEGIC NONRESPONSE

Strategic nonresponse consists of the conscious decision that, just for today (or even just for this one time) you will refrain from responding to whatever it is in your environment that annoys you or is causing you anxiety. For example, perhaps your boss is someone whose very presence causes you stress. Even worse, he or she has a habit of showing up unannounced, saying something critical (kind words or praise are just not in this person's vocabulary), and assigning you several new projects with seemingly impossible due dates.

In the past, you've found that you weren't able to focus your energy on what needs to be done after one of these encounters. You would find yourself simultaneously worried, depressed, angry, hurt, and immobilized. You tried all the other strategies we've explored in this book, but none of them worked for you. In this kind of situation, strategic nonresponse may be your best coping mechanism.

How the technique works is like this. Suppose that it's Tuesday morning at 10:15 and you've just had one of these encounters with your boss. Open your calendar and find an open time a few days in the future, such as Friday afternoon at 3:30. Record the following in your calendar: "Have a meltdown." Then decide in a very deliberate manner that, for this one occasion, you're going to refrain from having an emotional response.

Anytime in which you're tempted to give in to anxiety, anger, or despair, simply look at your calendar and say to yourself, "Oops. It's not Friday at 3:30. It's not time for my meltdown yet." Then return to dealing with your work in as productive a manner as possible.

When Friday at 3:30 comes, then go ahead: Give in to your feelings. Wallow in them. Feel as sorry for yourself as you like for as long as you scheduled the "appointment." If you had set aside fifteen minutes on your calendar, then indulge in your emotions and give yourself permission to feel as awful as you need to for a quarter of an hour. If you had set aside thirty minutes, then give in to these feelings for the full half hour.

But here's the secret of strategic nonresponse: In roughly 90 percent of the cases you use it, you won't need to keep that appointment. (And that's an added benefit: You just freed up some time on your calendar that you didn't know you were going to have.) By the time your scheduled meltdown is supposed to take place, you'll be feeling differently and might even be amused that you once thought you'd need that much time to feel bad about something that, in retrospect, wasn't really that big of an issue.

A variant of strategic nonresponse is a technique that I call *Bless and Release*. With this approach, when someone does something rude or annoying—cutting you off in traffic, neglecting to thank you for a significant favor you performed, making a rude gesture toward you when you didn't do anything wrong, and the like—rather than reacting, you simply smile and decide to let it go.

Maybe the person acted that way because he or she was having a bad day. In such a case, that person needs our sympathy and kindness more than our frustration or anger. Or maybe the person acted that way because he or she is simply a shallow, self-centered, ill-mannered person. In that case, that person needs our sympathy and kindness even more because he or she has to spend twenty-four hours a day in his or her own unpleasant company, and we don't. It's better to wish people like that well and send them on their way than permit them to increase our stress levels for even a moment.

CRITICAL ANALYSIS

The technique of critical analysis involves forcing ourselves to examine an emotion rather than merely feel it. When we realize that we're anxious, worried, overwhelmed, frustrated, or angry, we simply pause for a moment, identify the emotion that we're feeling, and then acknowledge it with a phrase like "Oh, so this is what it's like to feel . . . " or "Now I'm aware that I'm . . ."

This coping mechanism is particularly effective for those of us who work in higher education because we're so familiar with using our skills of critical analysis in our own research. In our scholarship, we're aware that we have to be skeptical of feelings and first impressions; we know we have to wait and see where the evidence takes us. The technique of critical analysis merely transfers this approach from our scholarship to the other aspects of our professional and personal lives.

For example, the stress we feel in our jobs is often increased by thoughts like the following:

- "He made me so angry."
- "She's so unreasonable that it makes me frustrated."
- "Their recklessness made me so tense."

With critical analysis, we remember to examine the evidence and see whether our conclusions are justified. Did his, her, or their action really *make* you angry, frustrated, or tense, or did he, she, or they do something, and then you chose (consciously or not) to have that emotional reaction? Are you really so victimized by what another person says or does that you have no control over your response?

In many cases, by critically analyzing the situation, you can realize that you do have other options. You can be amused, indifferent, compassionate, understanding, resolute, or a wide range of other possibilities. You don't *have* to respond as you previously thought you had to.

FOCUSING ON GRATITUDE

The next coping mechanism that we'll explore involves a technique for getting out of your own little world of personal concerns and anxieties by recognizing the good work that others are doing. By focusing on gratitude, we shift our thoughts from the negative and personal to the positive and communal.

The way in which you demonstrate appreciation to others depends on the particular type of stress that you're experiencing. For example, if what you're facing is a severe and ongoing challenge, then your expression of gratitude might take the form of one of those Serene Moments that we discussed earlier. Take five minutes off from whatever task is occupying you at the time, and write a brief note or make a short phone call to thank someone for having done something right.

You not only make that person's day better, but you also improve your own. You remind yourself that not everything that's happening around you is threatening and awful; other people are doing important work, and they like to know that you recognize it. When you return to your task five minutes later, you'll probably notice that it seems a little less overwhelming—and sometimes it can seem a lot less overwhelming—than it did before you took time to express gratitude to someone.

Another good habit to get into that will help you cope with stress more effectively is to *thank one more person a day than you ordinarily do*. Everyone has his or her own "rhythms of gratitude." Some people seem to thank almost everyone for almost anything. Other people rarely, if ever, express gratitude toward others. And most people fall somewhere in between those extremes.

The goal isn't to shift where you are on that scale radically but merely to add one more moment of gratitude to your day. Although the effect this practice has on your stress may not be instantaneous, it does occur rather quickly. After only a few weeks of thanking one more person each day who ordinarily would have gone unrecognized in your busy schedule, you'll start to find it easier to cope with the ordinary stresses and irritations of your job. The workplace will seem a calmer, less pressurized environment, and your positive attitude may even inspire a few of your coworkers to demonstrate a bit more gratitude themselves.

REWRITE YOUR PERSONAL MOVIE

As we've seen throughout this book, our bodies initiate the stress response whenever we perceive a threat. In many cases, that threat is self-inflicted. We cause ourselves anguish by repeating the same negative thoughts over and over—regrets, feelings of inadequacy, fears about the future, anxiety about things we can't control, and so on. These thoughts become our personal movies, and we run them on an endless loop in our heads. But if you really hated an actual movie, you wouldn't keep watching it, would you? So, why do you do so in the case of your own personal movies—these mental movies—that you keep reviewing over and over?

The alternative is to rewrite your personal movie. Rescript a humiliating moment as a story of personal growth and discovery. Recast a story of yourself as a victim to one in which you're a heroic survivor. Redirect a story of anxiety about the future so that it is instead an exciting adventure.

Doing so initially sounds hard, but it's actually much easier than it appears. Remember: Those thoughts that you keep running in your head aren't real experiences, even though your stress response *treats* them as actual experiences; they're just thoughts. And if your mind is capable of thinking thoughts that bring you anxiety, your mind is also capable of thinking thoughts that bring you joy, hope, and confidence.

In our earlier discussions of mindfulness and meditation, we saw that it's much better to rest our awareness in the present moment than in the past or future. But if, for whatever reason, you find your mind drawn to the past or future anyway, why not be aware of a pleasant experience instead of a painful one? After all, they're *your* thoughts. Do what you want with them.

FINAL THOUGHTS ABOUT COPING WITH STRESS

As with any strategy for dealing with stress, different coping mechanisms work better for certain people in certain situations than they do for others. Some academic leaders find that an occasional Serene Moment in their own Serene Refuge is all they need to help them deal with the stresses they can't otherwise embrace, reduce, or manage. Others discover that critically analyzing a situation and choosing to engage in Strategic Nonresponse are their best alternatives.

The most important thing to keep in mind when nothing else seems to work in addressing your stress is that you have resources. In fact, you have a lot of them. Pick up this book again and try an approach that may not have been particularly effective in the past but that now may be suitable for your current situation. Scan the list of resources at the end of this book and select other guides that may give you even more tools for your stress management toolkit. See if your college or university has an Employee Assistance Program that can help you deal with stress.

Whatever option you choose, the point is that you're not alone in your need to cope with stress more effectively, and there are lots of guides and people who can assist you. When it comes to the stress of being an academic leader, just knowing that we're all in this together can often be the best mechanism for coping with stress that there is.

Any one of the techniques we've considered is useful, in and of itself, for helping administrators deal with the pressures of their jobs. Nevertheless, in order to gain the maximum possible effect of all these stress management techniques, it's necessary to combine them into a comprehensive strategy for dealing with the challenges academic leaders face in managing their time and stress simultaneously. And the best ways of combining time management and stress management into a single, holistic approach will provide the focus of our concern in the final two chapters of this book.

Part III

PUTTING IT ALL TOGETHER

Chapter 17

A Holistic Approach to Managing Time and Stress

The final step in putting together a strategy for managing time and stress is making sure that all the pieces fit together for you. Rarely do people find that only one of the techniques we've explored in this book addresses their stress adequately and completely in every situation. A more holistic approach to stress requires us to prepare a toolkit of approaches that are likely to be effective for us in various scenarios.

That's why it's so helpful to have a good sense of what your stress triggers are, which of these triggers increase your stress level, and which of them spike your stress level. (Review the exercise we did in chapter 14.) In that way, you can be prepared as soon as you notice that one of these triggers is occurring and adopt the tool that's most likely to help you in that particular situation.

A good way of thinking of stress management holistically is to think of it as similar to whatever type of natural disaster—hurricanes, earthquakes, tornadoes, wildfires, and the like—most commonly affects the area in which you live. The most sensible approach is not to wait for the disaster to occur but to have a plan ready for what you'll do if an emergency should occur. In many cases, that planning includes having supplies on hand to get you through the disaster. It's better to have those supplies and not need them than to need them and not have them.

Your stress management plan works in much the same way. It includes advance consideration of what you'll do in situations when you feel your stress is increasing and the supplies you'll need if you find yourself in a situation you can't handle.

Your advance consideration involves identifying the strategies and techniques of dealing with stress that we've explored. Your supply kit includes your list of resources: access to your institution's Employee Assistance Plan if you have one, the phone number of a counselor or trusted advisor you can talk to, objects or images that you find useful in helping you relieve your stress in a safe and healthy manner, and so on.

In many cases, you may discover that simply having a stress management plan is the best stress management strategy you can adopt. It can calm you down in particularly difficult situations by reminding you that you've prepared for this eventuality and have considered what you're going to do next.

PROPER VENTILATION

One strategy often recommended to academic leaders that definitely *doesn't* work is venting to "release the pressure" of the stress they're under. Venting can involve anything from punching a pillow to engaging in a "primal scream," but none of these strategies is effective. Since stress is the body's natural response to a perceived threat, any activity you engage in when you try to "let it all out" only causes your nervous system to relive the stress trigger all over again. In fact, many people find that attempts to vent the pressure that they're under actually ends up making them feel more tense and anxious than they were before.

Similar experiences can occur if you try to vent your stress by sharing your concerns with someone else. Although a loved one will certainly want to know what's troubling you, it's counterproductive to discuss the stress you're under with too many people. Each time you tell your story, you mentally relive the stress trigger. Moreover, you many end up increasing the stress level of the person you're talking to with the result that, rather than solving your own problem, you retain it and simultaneously create a new problem for someone else.

The most productive alternative to venting stress is to process your feelings through writing. Either on paper or in a word processing document, explore your sense of stress as candidly and objectively as you can. How does the stress make you feel? What are you ultimately concerned will happen? Why does that outcome disturb you? Writing out your concerns in this way tends to be most effective when you do it several days in a row without concern for repeating yourself or taking the time to correct your spelling or grammar.

Then, after "purging" your stress for five or six days in this way, shred what you've written or delete the file. That final step accomplishes two goals at once: It reduces the likelihood that anyone will ever read these very personal notes you've written, and there is something therapeutic about the act of eliminating a document that contains all your stressful thoughts. It can feel almost as though you're obliterating your stress through the act of obliterating your description of that stress.

WHY LAUGHTER REALLY IS THE BEST MEDICINE

If you've ever had a really stressful day at work only to find yourself forgetting about your concerns (at least temporarily) when someone tells you a really funny story or when you watch a good comedy on television, you already know the power that laughter has over stress. Humor takes our thoughts beyond our own immediate concerns, reminds us that not everything in life is serious, and helps us release the tension in our bodies.

You can even recreate some of this effect merely by forcing yourself to smile during a moment of great stress. (You may want to try doing so when you're alone, however; otherwise, a sudden broad smile during a moment that may be stressful for others, too, may be misinterpreted.) It's quite difficult to remain immersed in severe stress when you're smiling, even when you're *forcing* yourself to smile, so genuine, spontaneous laughter has an even more profound effect.

For this reason, every academic leader's approach to stress management should include efforts to find at least some humor in the world and in his or her work, no matter how serious the issues he or she may be addressing. When an academic leader gets home from work after a hard day, it's a good idea to

- exchange with others lighter, more positive stories about the day rather than reliving all the tension that occurred during the day,
- watch lighthearted movies such as romantic comedies instead of suspense thrillers that can keep the nervous system in a state of high alert, and
- read books that are more motivational or inspirational in nature rather than prose that causes an impending sense of dread or that doesn't allow the reader to get his or her mind off of work.

It's not that academic leaders have to change their taste in books, movies, and conversational topics forever. By following this advice, they'd merely be taking a short break from the sort of fare that could increase their level of stress at a time when they need to relieve it, not relive it.

FOCUSING ON WHAT'S IMPORTANT

When we were addressing time management in chapter 3, we saw the importance of distinguishing obligations that are important from those that are merely urgent. Important tasks have *significance*; they'll matter to us and our programs long after they're completed. Urgent tasks only have *tight deadlines*; within a few days or a few months at most, they'll probably be forgotten.

That same redirection of focus on things that are important and that truly matter also helps us understand the point at which time management and stress management begin to merge. In other words, we tend to feel less stressed when we feel that we're making progress toward an important goal. Moving toward a significant objective takes our minds off the day-to-day frustrations of our work and reminds us why those frustrations are worthwhile.

When pressures build and our workload increases, our natural tendency is to focus our energies on our most immediate problems rather than our longer-term goals. But, in many ways, this type of short-term thinking is exactly the opposite of what we should be doing. Stressful times can be handled more effectively—and, in terms of time management, more *efficiently*—when we are mindful of those tasks that will matter to the greatest number of people or that are likely to remain significant several years from now as opposed to those that cry out for our attention because a deadline is looming or because their "wheels" are the "squeakiest."

In other words, good time management *is* good stress management in a number of important ways:

- By remaining mindful of our core values and most important goals, we achieve a greater number of our highest priorities at the same time that we feel less pressured by all the petty tasks that seem to be imposed on us from all sides.
- By making sure that we're guided by the compass of our values and priorities, we can take comfort in knowing that we're getting the *right* things done in the *right* order instead of wasting our time rushing ineffectively from problem to problem.
- By having our own workspaces organized in a time-efficient manner, we also create the sort of environment that calms our nerves and helps us to deal more effectively with the challenges we face. Messy work areas aren't just inefficient; they also cause us to become anxious and make our thoughts more disorganized.

In the 1960s and 1970s, a common figure on the variety show circuit was a performer known as Erich Brenn. His entire act was spinning plates, cups, and bowls, either directly on a table or atop long, thin poles. To put this in other terms: Erich Brenn's entire job was to rush frantically from place to place, making sure that everything didn't come crashing down around him. At the end of his performance, an audience member might have been tempted to say, "That was all very impressive. But what in the world did it really accomplish?"

Academic leaders sometimes suffer from what we might call Erich Brenn syndrome. They, too, rush from place to place, solving one problem after another, and trying to keep everything from crashing down around them. And at the end of their careers, they may be tempted to say, "That was all very exhausting. But what in the world did it really accomplish?"

A comprehensive approach to managing time and stress helps prevent us from experiencing Erich Brenn syndrome. It's less exhausting because it avoids the frantic rushing around to solve endless series of problems. It's not reactive. It isn't even just proactive. It's transformative in that it changes weary, frenzied academic leaders into calmer, more effective administrators at the same time that it renovates their programs so as to improve the quality of learning, research, and innovation that occurs.

TAKING A HOLISTIC VIEW

A holistic approach to managing time and stress thus consists of giving due consideration to all three domains of our lives—body, mind, and spirit—while using the ten primary strategies of time management (chapters 2–11) and the four primary strategies of stress management (chapters 13–16) that we've explored in this book.

- With regard to your *body*, remember that the time you take for exercise is not a distraction from your commitment to manage your time and stress more effectively; it's a vital part of that program. Get enough sleep, eat a well-balanced diet, drink plenty of water, cut down on caffeinated beverages, and be sure that you're receiving adequate amounts of the vitamins that help your body deal with stress, including B-complex vitamins such as B1 (thiamine), B3 (niacin), and B6 (pyridoxine). If you're having trouble falling asleep, many people find that moderate, short-term use of melatonin or valerian root helps restore their bodies' natural sleep cycles. And those sleep cycles will help recharge your personal energy cycle (see chapter 5).
- With regard to your *mind*, start viewing mental relaxation and reflection as just as important as physical exercise. Both help you become more productive during those times when you're actually working and enable you to cope with the pressures of your work most effectively. Don't add to your mental stress by continuing to criticize yourself for past mistakes that can't be rectified or by blaming others for the wrongs they did you. Those angry thoughts you harbor interfere with your own ability to deal with stress more than they affect the person who caused you grief.
- With regard to your *spirit*, explore the ways in which the work that you do and the discomfort that is an unavoidable part of your work are meaningful.

If you are religious, mentally offer your suffering as a sacrifice. If you have a more secular worldview, regard the triggers of your stress as opportunities for personal growth. Identify the values that you personally regard as important, and ask yourself whether yielding to stress is helping you live up to those values in a time-efficient manner. If it is not, then challenge yourself to embody your core values more fully. Resist any attempts to see yourself as a victim in any stressful situation, and view yourself instead as strong enough to endure any tests that your job and personal life may present you.

And then, in accordance with the principles outlined in this book, apply the strategies summarized in Figure 17.1, and you'll be better prepared for the sort of trials that are inevitable in any position of academic leadership.

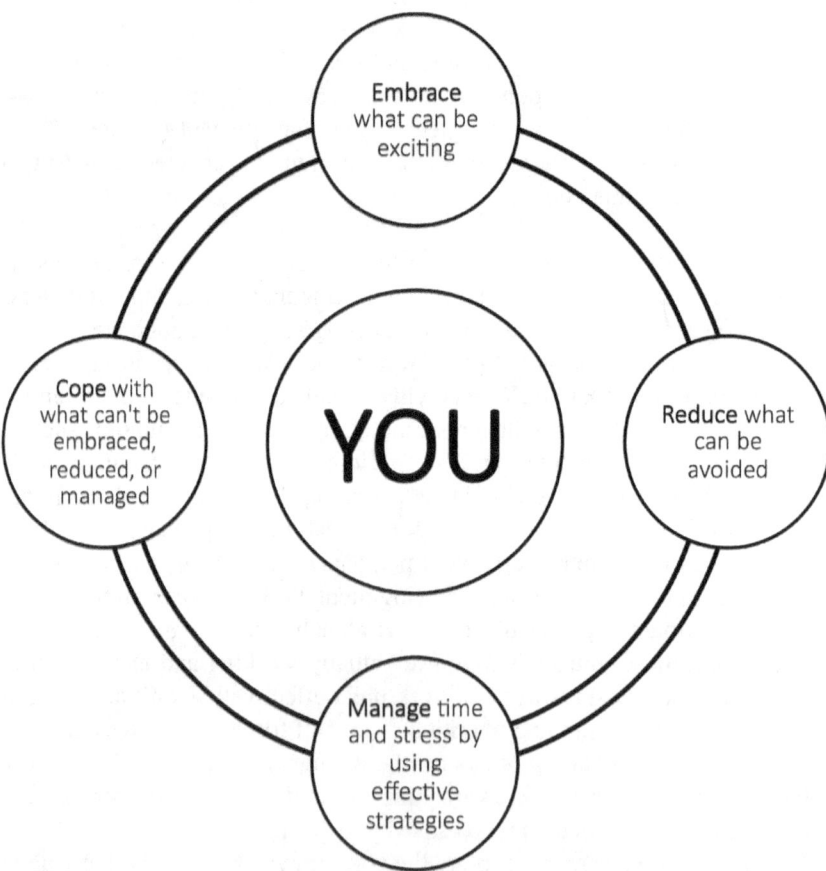

Figure 17.1

As one last component of a holistic approach to managing time and stress, therefore, the following *punch list* (i.e., a set of standardized operating procedures that is used to make certain that all key steps have been completed) can be useful in helping you keep your priorities straight.

- I am mindful of the reasons why I became an academic leader in the first place.
- I am mindful of the most important goals I would like to achieve in my current position.
- I am mindful of the most important goals I would like to achieve within the next twelve months.
- I am mindful of how I should be structuring my time so as to achieve my most important goals.
- I am mindful of the specific reasons why I may be experiencing stress at the moment.
- I am mindful of how the stressful situation or environment I'm in relates to the reasons why I became an academic leader in the first place or brings me closer to my professional goals.
- I am mindful of how I should avoid permitting this level of stress to distract me from pursuit of my most important goals in a timely manner.

In many cases, reflecting on *why* you're working in a stressful environment will help you to *endure* that stressful environment and allow you to continue working more efficiently. The discomfort of the stress and the demands on your time becomes, in short, less like the pain of an injury and more like the soreness of healing.

Chapter 18

Academic Leaders as Role Models

Almost every leadership development program, whether designed for academic administrators or otherwise, at some point discusses the differences between leadership and management. People quote some of Warren Bennis's famous observations, such as "The manager maintains; the leader develops," "The manager asks how and when; the leader asks what and why," or (most commonly) "The manager does things right; the leader does the right thing" (Bennis, 2009, 42).

The basic idea is that management is about making sure that things are done efficiently, policies are followed, and attention is paid to both budgets and deadlines; leadership is about making sure that things are done effectively, new visions are created, and attention is paid to both people and their individual growth.

By these standards, dealing with time and stress is obviously a *management* activity. We're in the realm of conserving resources when we try to allocate our time properly and cope with the stresses of our positions. Even the names given to these activities—time *management*, stress *management*—suggest that they don't fall under the heading of leadership. But as we reach our conclusion in this book, it may be worth asking whether there might be such a thing as time and stress *leadership*.

I think that there is indeed a place for such a concept. *Leaders set the tone for the areas they lead.* When department chairs or deans constantly look frazzled, always seem to be under pressure from the amount of work they have to perform, and indulge in *thriving on busy* (see chapter 11), they serve as a poor example to others. Good time management strategies demonstrate members of the faculty and staff can improve their own efficiency.

When the person in charge is in a positive mood, it reduces the stress of everyone who works in that area, while simultaneously increasing productivity and promoting employee retention. Members of an office, department, or program tend to share moods, whether positive or negative, and we have to remember that positive moods are often associated with increased performance. So, as an academic leader, dealing effectively with time and stress isn't just essential for your own success; it's also essential to the success of the people who work with you.

In conclusion, therefore, what time and stress leadership consists of includes

- serving as an expert role model in meeting priorities and handling the pressures commonly found in leadership positions at colleges and universities today,
- discovering new, more efficient processes that allow people to accomplish more in less time, and
- slashing red tape where possible by eliminating redundancy, consolidating forms, and condensing bureaucratic levels.

No system we can devise as academic leaders will ever eliminate all the pressure we're under or make our work easy, but if you are diligent in applying the concepts described in this book, you will be well positioned to deal with all the challenges of time and stress that may come your way.

Resources on Time and Stress Management for Academic Leaders

Abouserie, R. (1996). Stress, coping strategies and job satisfaction in university academic staff. *Educational Psychology, 16*(1), 49–56.

Adams, S. (2014). *How to fail at almost everything and still win big: Kind of the story of my life*. New York: Portfolio.

Allen, D. (2001). *Getting things done: The art of stress-free productivity*. New York: Viking Penguin.

Anderson, J. (2006). *A weekend to change your life: Find your authentic self after a lifetime of being all things to all people*. New York: Broadway Books.

Arnold, C. L. (2014). *Small move, big change: Using microresolutions to transform your life permanently*. New York: Penguin Books.

Bakke, D. W. (2005). *Joy at work: A revolutionary approach to fun on the job*. Seattle, WA: PVG.

Bennis, W. G. (2009). *On becoming a leader* (Twentieth anniversary edition). New York: Basic Books.

Berg, M., and Seeber, B. K. (2016). *The slow professor: Challenging the culture of speed in the academy*. Toronto, CAN: University of Toronto Press.

Berry, J. F. (2010). *Organize now! A week-by-week guide to simplify your space and your life*. Cincinnati, OH: Betterway Home.

Berry, J. F. (2011). *Organize now! Your money, business & career*. Blue Ash, OH: Betterway Home.

Berry, J. F. (2013). *Organize now! Think & live clutter-free*. Blue Ash, OH: Betterway Home.

Brantley, J., and Millstine, W. (2007). *Five good minutes at work: 100 mindful practices to help you relieve stress & bring your best to work*. Oakland, CA: New Harbinger.

Buck, F. (2016). *Get organized!: Time management for school leaders*. New York: Routledge.

Buller, J. L. (2011). *Academic leadership day by day: Small steps that lead to great success*. San Francisco, CA: Jossey-Bass.

CareerTrack. (2006). *Taking control of your workday: How to achieve more in less time—with less stress* [CD and downloadable workbook]. United States of America: CareerTrack.

CareerTrack. (2008). *Templates for today's time-crunched professional* [CD and downloadable workbook]. United States of America: CareerTrack.

Chapman, G., White, P., and Myra, H. (2014). *Rising above a toxic workplace: Taking care of yourself in an unhealthy environment*. Chicago, IL: Northfield.

Claessens, B. J. C., van Eerde, W., Rutte, C. G., and Roe, R. A. (2007). A review of the time management literature. *Personnel Review, 36*(2), 255–276. https://doi.org/10.1108/00483480710726136.

Covey, S. R. (1989). *The 7 habits of highly effective people: Powerful lessons in personal change*. New York: Simon & Schuster.

Covey, S. R. (2015). *First things first*. Salt Lake City, UT: Franklin Covey.

Crandell, G. (2005). Time management for more effective results. *The Department Chair, 15*(3), 11–12.

Critchley, K. (2010). *Stress management skills training course: Exercises and techniques to manage stress and anxiety*. Lancashire, UK: Universe of Learning.

Crookston, R. K. (2012). *Working with problem faculty: A 6-step guide for department chairs*. San Francisco, CA: Jossey-Bass.

Crowley, K., and Elster, K. (2006). *Working with you is killing me: Freeing yourself from emotional traps at work*. New York: Grand Central.

David, S. (2016). *Emotional agility: Get unstuck, embrace change, and thrive in work and life*. Garden City, NY: Avery.

Dean, J. (2013). *Making habits, breaking habits: Why we do things, why we don't, and how to make any change stick*. Philadelphia, PA: DaCapo.

Doran, G., Miller, A., and Cunningham, C. (1981, November). There's a S.M.A.R.T. way to write management's goals and objectives. *Management Review, 70*(11), 35–36.

Dore, M. (2017, June 13). Why you should manage your energy, not your time. *BBC*. Retrieved from http://www.bbc.com/capital/story/20170612-why-you-should-manage-your-energy-not-your-time.

Duhigg, C. (2014). *The power of habit: Why we do what we do in life and business*. New York: Random House Trade Paperbacks.

Duhigg, C. (2017). *Smarter faster better: The transformative power of real productivity*. New York: Random House Trade Paperbacks.

Dweck, C. S. (2008). *Mindset: The new psychology of success*. New York: Ballantine Books.

Emmons, H. (2010). *The chemistry of calm: A powerful, drug-free plan to quiet your fears and overcome your anxiety*. New York: Touchstone.

Fred Pryor Seminars. (2005). *How to manage multiple projects, meet deadlines, & achieve objectives* [CD]. United States of America: Fred Pryor Seminars.

Gawande, A. (2009). *The checklist manifesto: How to get things right*. New York: Picador.

Gillespie, N. A., Walsh, M., Winefield, A. H., Dua, J., and Stough, C. (2001). Occupational stress in universities: Staff perceptions of the causes, consequences and moderators of stress. *Work & Stress, 15*(1), 53–72.

Glei, J. K. (ed.). (2013). *Manage your day-to-day: Build your routine, find your focus, and sharpen your creative mind.* Las Vegas, NV: Amazon.

Gmelch, W. H. (1982). *Beyond stress to effective management.* New York: Wiley.

Gmelch, W. H. (1993). *Coping with faculty stress.* Newbury Park, CA: Sage.

Gmelch, W. H., and Burns, J. S. (1993). The cost of academic leadership: Department chair stress. *Innovative Higher Education, 17*(4), 259–270.

Gmelch, W. H., and Chan, W. (1992). *Administrator stress and coping effectiveness: A transactional study.* Washington, DC: ERIC Clearinghouse.

Gmelch, W. H., and Miskin, V. D. (1993). *Leadership skills for department chairs.* Bolton, MA: Anker.

Greenberg, M. (2014, April 15). 6 ways to turn bad stress into good stress. *Alternet.* Retrieved from http://www.alternet.org/6-ways-turn-bad-stress-good-stress.

Guilmartin, N. (2010). *The power of pause: How to be more effective in a demanding, 24/7 world.* San Francisco, CA: Jossey-Bass.

Hansen, C. K. (2011). *Time management for department chairs.* San Francisco, CA: Jossey-Bass.

Heath, C., and Heath, D. (2013). *Switch: How to change things when change is hard.* New York: Random House.

Held, B. (2001). *Stop smiling, start kvetching: A 5-step guide to creative complaining.* New York: St. Martin's Press.

Herman, K. C., and Reinke, W. M. (2014). *Stress management for teachers: A proactive guide.* New York: The Guilford Press.

Heyck-Merlin, M. (2016). *The together leader: Get organized for your success—and sanity!: A guide for school-based, district, and nonprofit leaders.* San Francisco, CA: Jossey-Bass.

Jonat, R. (2014). *Do less: A minimalist guide to a simplified, organized, and happy life.* Avon, MA: Adams Media.

Kashdan, T., and Biswas-Diener, R. (2015). *The upside of your dark side: Why being your whole self—not just your "good" self—drives success and fulfillment.* New York: Plume.

Kirschner, R., and Brinkman, R. (1999). *Life by design: Making wise choices in a mixed-up world.* New York: McGraw-Hill.

Kogon, K., Merrill, A., and Rinne, L. (2014). *The 5 choices: The path to extraordinary productivity.* New York: Simon & Schuster.

Kondo, M. (2014). *The life-changing magic of tidying up: The Japanese art of decluttering and organizing.* New York: Potter/TenSpeed/Harmony.

Kruse, K. (2015). *15 secrets successful people know about time management: The productivity habits of 7 billionaires, 13 Olympic athletes, 29 straight-a students, and 239 entrepreneurs.* Phoenix, AZ: The Kruse Group.

Leeds, R. (2000). *The zen of organizing: Creating order and peace in your home, career, and life.* Los Angeles, CA: Park Slope Press.

Leeds, R. (2008). *One year to an organized life: From your closets to your finances, the week-by-week guide to getting completely organized for good.* Cambridge, MA: Da Capo Press.

Leeds, R. (2009). *One year to an organized work life: From your desk to your deadlines, the week-by-week guide to eliminating office stress for good.* Cambridge, MA: Da Capo Press.

Leeds, R. (2012). *The 8 minute organizer: Easy solutions to simplify your life in your spare time.* Boston, MA: Da Capo Press.

Lewis, M. M. (2003). *Moneyball: The art of winning an unfair game.* New York: Norton.

Loehr, J. E., and Schwartz, T. (2005). *The power of full engagement: Managing energy, not time, is the key to high performance and personal renewal.* New York: Free Press.

Lyubomirsky, S. (2008). *The how of happiness: A new approach to getting the life you want.* New York: Penguin Books.

Lyubomirsky, S. (2013). *The myths of happiness: What should make you happy, but doesn't, what shouldn't make you happy, but does.* New York: Penguin.

Macan, T. H. (1996). Time-management training: Effects on time behaviors, attitudes, and job performance. *The Journal of Psychology, 130*(3), 229–236. http://dx.doi.org/10.1080/00223980.1996.9915004.

Maravelas, A. (2005). *How to reduce workplace conflict and stress: How leaders and their employees can protect their sanity and productivity from tension and turf wars.* Pompton Plains, NJ: The Career Press.

Maxwell, J. C. (2000). *Failing forward: Turning mistakes into stepping stones for success.* Nashville, TN: Nelson Books.

May, J. R., and McBeath, R. B. (1993). *Enhancing departmental leadership: The roles of the chairperson.* Lanham, MD: Rowman & Littlefield.

McMillan, M. (2009). *Pink bat: Turning problems into solutions.* Naperville, IL: Simple Truths.

Melnick, S. (2013). *Success under stress: Powerful tools for staying calm, confident, and productive when the pressure's on.* New York: Amacom.

O'Connor, R. (2015). *Rewire: Change your brain to break bad habits, overcome addictions, conquer self-destructive behavior.* New York: Plume/Random House.

Oettingen, G. (2014). *Rethinking positive thinking: Inside the new science of motivation.* New York: Penguin.

Pollan, S. M., and Levin, M. (1996). *Lifescripts: What to say to get what you want in 101 of life's toughest situations.* New York: Hungry Minds.

Pollay, D. J. (2010). *The law of the garbage truck: How to stop people from dumping on you.* New York: Sterling.

Ricard, M. (2007). *Happiness: A guide to developing life's most important skill.* Translated by J. Browner. New York: Little, Brown and Company. (Original work published 2003).

Roos, D. (2016). *Don't read this book: Time management for creative people.* Amsterdam, NLD: BIS.

Sarros, J. C., Wolverton, M., Gmelch, W. H., and Wolverton, M. L. (1999). Stress in academic leadership: U.S. and Australian department chairs/heads. *The Review of Higher Education, 22*(2), 165–185.

Scott, S. J. (2014). *To-do list makeover: A simple guide to getting the important things done*. (n.p.): Archangel Ink.

Scott, S. J., and Davenport, B. (2016). *Declutter your mind: How to stop worrying, relieve anxiety, and eliminate negative thinking*. Cranbury, NJ: Oldtown.

Seldin, P. (1987). *Coping with faculty stress*. San Francisco, CA: Jossey-Bass.

Seligman, M. E. P. (2006). *Learned optimism: How to change your mind and your life*. New York: Vintage.

Seligman, M. E. P. (2013). *Flourish: A visionary new understanding of happiness and well-being*. New York: Atria.

Smith, M. J. (1975). *When I say no, I feel guilty*. New York: Bantam Books.

Stahl, B., and Goldstein, E. (2010). *A mindfulness-based stress reduction workbook*. Oakland, CA: New Harbinger.

Stahl, B., Meleo-Meyer, F., and Koerbel, L. (2014). *A mindfulness-based stress reduction workbook for anxiety*. Oakland, CA: New Harbinger.

Tracy, B. (2017). *Eat that frog!: 21 great ways to stop procrastinating and get more done in less time*. Oakland, CA: Berrett-Koehler.

Tytherleigh, M. Y., Webb, C., Cooper, C. L., and Ricketts, C. (2005). Occupational stress in UK higher education institutions: A comparative study of all staff categories. *Higher Education Research & Development, 24*(1), 41–61.

Webb, C. (2016). *How to have a good day: Harness the power of behavioral science to transform your working life*. New York: Crown Business.

Wells, C. M. (2016). *Mindfulness: How school leaders can reduce stress and thrive on the job*. Lanham, MD: Rowman & Littlefield.

Williams, K., and Reid, M. (2011). *Time management: Pocket study skills*. New York: Palgrave Macmillan.

Yackle, K., Schwarz, L. A., Kam, K., Sorokin, J. M., Huguenard, J. R., Feldman, J. L., . . . Krasnow, M. A. (2017). Breathing control center neurons that promote arousal in mice. *Science, 355*(6332), 1411–1415.

More about ATLAS

ATLAS: Academic Training, Leadership, & Assessment Services offers training programs, books, and materials dealing with collegiality and positive academic leadership. Its more than fifty highly interactive programs include the following:

- Introduction to Academic Leadership
- Team Building for Academic Leaders
- Time Management for Academic Leaders
- Stress Management for Academic Leaders
- Budgeting for Academic Leaders
- Decision Making for Academic Leaders
- Problem Solving for Academic Leaders
- Conflict Management for Academic Leaders
- Emotional Intelligence for Academic Leaders
- Effective Communication for Academic Leaders
- Work–Life Balance for Academic Leaders
- Best Practices in Academic Fund-Raising
- Protecting Yourself from a Toxic Work Environment
- Developing Leadership Capacity: How You Can Create a Leadership Development Program at Your Institution
- We've Got to Stop Meeting Like This: Leading Meetings Effectively
- Why Academic Leaders Must Lead Differently: Understanding the Organizational Culture of Higher Education
- Getting Organized: Taking Control of Your Schedule, Workspace, and Habits to Get More Done in Less Time with Lower Stress
- Collegiality and Teambuilding

- Change Leadership in Higher Education
- Promoting Faculty and Staff Engagement
- Best Practices in Faculty Recruitment and Hiring
- Best Practices in Faculty Evaluation
- Best Practices in Coaching and Mentoring
- Moving Forward: Training and Development for Advisory Boards
- Training the Trainers: How to Give Presentations and Provide Training the ATLAS Way
- Managing Up for Academic Leaders: How to Flourish When Dealing with Your Boss and Your Boss's Boss
- Creating a Culture of Student Success
- Positive Academic Leadership: How to Stop Putting Out Fires and Start Making a Difference
- Authentic Academic Leadership: A Values-Based Approach to Academic Leadership
- Mindful Academic Leadership: A Mindfulness-Based Approach to Academic Leadership
- Fostering a College University: An In-Depth Exploration of Collegiality in Higher Education
- Managing Conflict: An In-Depth Exploration of Conflict Management in Higher Education
- A Toolkit for College Professors
- A Toolkit for Department Chairs
- Exploring Academic Leadership: Is College/University Administration Right for Me?

ATLAS offers programs in half-day, full-day, and multiday formats. ATLAS also offers reduced prices on leadership books and sells materials that can be used to assess your institution or program:

- The Collegiality Assessment Matrix (CAM), which allows academic programs to evaluate the collegiality and civility of their faculty members in a consistent, objective, and reliable manner
- The Self-Assessment Matrix (S-AM), which is a self-evaluation version of the CAM
- The ATLAS Campus Climate and Morale Survey
- The ATLAS Faculty and Staff Engagement Survey

These assessment instruments are available in both electronic and paper formats. In addition, the ATLAS E-Newsletter addresses a variety of issues related to academic leadership and is sent free to subscribers.

For more information, contact:

ATLAS: Academic Training, Leadership, & Assessment Services
9154 Wooden Road
Raleigh, NC 27617
800–355–6742; www.atlasleadership.com
E-mail: questions@atlasleadership.com

Index

academic leadership: accountability of, 4; goals of, 12; growth mind-set of, 87, 90–91; habits of, 53, 67–68; management *vs.*, 139; positive mood of, 139–40; resources of, 19–24, 48, 126, 131; as role models, 140; task priority of, 5, 44; workload of, 3–4, 115

academic year, lacking time in, 4–5

accomplishment, to-do list for, 41, 42–43, 46

accountability, of academic leadership, 4

adaptation. *See* general adaptation syndrome

Adobe Portable Document Format (PDF), 53

altitude model, for goals, 60

Anapana meditation. *See* Shamatha meditation

Appointments with Yourself, task clustering, 40, 43, 49

avoidance, of triggers, 93, 96, 101

the Bactrian camel (metaphor), 27, *27*, 38

balance, of stress level, 76–77

the battery (metaphor), *26*, 26–27, 38

benefits: of eustress, 87, 89–90; of massage, 107; of stress, 76–77, 88; of time log, 35–36; of to-do list, 41, 43

Bennis, Warren, 139

best practices, for goals, 58–60

black holes of time (metaphor): eliminating, 61, 64; habits as, 63–64; meetings as, 62–63

Bless and Release, 123

body, mind, spirit: holistic approach for, 135–36

"body clocks," 25

bottlenecks, documents causing, 47

breaks, from work, 121, 125

breathing exercises: smartphone apps for, 103; for stress management, 102–03. *See also* Shamatha meditation

Brenn, Erich, 134–35

Brewster's Millions, 7

Brewster's Millions Experiment, 7–9, 19

budget: of money, 7–9; for time management, 6, 9–12

calmness, 102–103, 106; environments of, 117–18; music for, 116–17

Cannon, Walter, 73, 83

change, commitment for, 57–58

Circadian Rhythms, 25

clarification: of goals, 55–57, 60; of tasks, 42

clinic, as task clustering, 39

151

clustering, of tasks, 38–40
cognitive restructuring, of predisposing triggers, 97–98
commitment: for change, 57–58; to tidy workspace, 51–52
communication, in nexus of resources, 20, *21*
compartmentalization, as lacking efficiency, 63
complex *vs.* simple, habits, 67
conscious thought, habits and, 65–66
continuous partial attention, 38
control, over triggers, 93–100
control and safety, 85–87
conversion, of documents, 52–53
coping mechanism: examining emotions as, 124; gratitude as, 124–25; mental shift as, 126–27; mental vacation as, 119–20; serene moment/refuge as, 120–22, 126; strategic nonresponse as, 122–23, 126
coping mechanisms, for stress, 119–26
cortisol effect, stress and, 74, 83
cost/benefit analysis, of meetings, 62
costs, opportunity *vs.* actual, 24
covert *vs.* overt: precipitating triggers and, 100; predisposing triggers and, 96–97
Covey, Stephen R.: *Seven Habits of Highly Effective People*, by, 14, 14–15, 65
creation: of mental vacation, 119–20; of serene moment/refuge, 120–22; of time log, 36–38
The *"Creative Minds Have Cluttered Desks" Fallacy*, 47–48
Cunningham, James, 55

data: from time log, 38; on time management, 6
Deadline/Payoff System, for to-do lists, 45
deadlines: fear of, 13; as flexible, 15; stress resulting from, 73, 76, 81; tasks driving, 13–15, 43

Dean, Jeremy: *Making Habits, Breaking Habits* by, 65, 67
deep breathing. *See* breathing exercises
demands, of stakeholders, 4, 47
desensitization, of predisposing triggers, 94–95
diet, for stress management, 79–80, 135–36
Disney, Walt, 68
documents: *bottleneck* of, 47; converting, 52–53; fallacies about, 47–48; OHIO Method for, 48–51; schedule for, 49, 51; sorting, 50–51
document scanner, 53
Doran, George, 55
Duhigg, Charles: *The Power of Habit* by, 65–67; *Smarter, Faster, Better* by, 65
Dweck, Carol: *Mindset* by, 90–91

efficiency: compartmentalization lacking, 63; energy cycle for, 30–31, 33–34; multitasking lacking, 38; obstacles to, 4–5, 47–48; time log for, 35–36, *36–37*, 38; "time puddles and lakes" and, 10; in urgent *vs.* important, 17
Einstein, Albert, 19
Eisenhower, Dwight D., 13–14
elimination: of black holes of time, 61, 64; of tasks, 16, 35
e-mail: as habit, 66–67; organizing, 49–50
e-mail time, time clustering for, 39–40, 49–50
Employee Assistance Program, 126, 131–32
energy cycles, personal, 67; efficiency through, 30–31, 33–34; exercise for, 29, 30, *31–33*; metaphors of, 25–28, *26*, *27*, *28*; tasks linked to, 28–31, *29*, 34, 35, 38–39; time management and, 28–34, 67
energy level: inventorying, 28–30, *29*, 30–31, *31–33*; personal cycle

of, 25; redirecting, 33–34, 134–35; stakeholders and, 28, 31–33; time log and, 37
engagement: with goals, 57–58; in work, 34, 135–36
enjoyment: of stress, 84–87, 89–90; of tasks, 68–69
environment, for stress management, 117–18
eustress: as beneficial, 87, 89–90; Selye on, 84–85, 87, 91
examination, of emotions: as coping mechanism, 124
exercise, for stress management, 79–80, 135–36
exercises: for energy cycle, *29*, 30, *31–33*; for gratitude, 115–16; for metta mindfulness, 113–15; for stress levels, *74–75*, 74–76, 77–79, *78*; for time budget, 7–10; for triggers, 94; urgent *vs.* important tasks, 15–16

faith, in God, 113–14
fallacies, about documents, 47–48
falsehoods, about meditation, 104
fear: of deadlines, 13; triggers and, 89, 96–97
fight-or-flight response, 73–74, 83
Fiverr, 22
flexibility, of deadlines, 15
the four quadrants, of Covey, *14*, 14–16
fund-raising, 3

general adaptation syndrome, 83–85
goals: of academic leadership, 12; altitude model for, 60; best practices for, 58–60; clarifying, 55–57, 60; engagement with, 57–58; prioritizing, 12, 35, 134; SMART and SMARTER, 55–58, *56*, *59*, 60
God, 113–14
gradual *vs.* all-at-once systems, 51–52, *52*
grant writing, 10, 14–15
gratitude: as coping mechanism, 124–25; exercises for, 115–16; increasing, 116, 125; journal for, 115; for stress management, 115–16
Greenberg, Melanie, 87–88, 90
growth mind-set, for stress management, 87, 90–91

habit cycle: cue, routine, reward as, 66, 68
habits: of academic leaders, 53, 67–68; as black holes of time, 63–64; conscious thought and, 65–66; of "highly effective people," 14–15, 65; keystone, 66–67; reprogramming, 65–67
"happy place," 120
Heath, Chip, 57
Heath, Dan, 57
holistic approach, 80, 82, 118, 127, 131, *136*; for body, mind, spirit, 135–36; humor and, 133; *punch list* for, 137; for venting stress, 132
humor, for stress management, 133

The "I Might Need This Someday" Fallacy, 47
increase, of gratitude, 116, 125
information, in nexus of resources, 20, *21*
intention-setting, 80
Internet, services on, 21–22
inventory: of energy, 28–30, *29*, 30–31, *31–33*; of meetings, 62; of stress, *74–75*, 74–76, 77–79, *78*, 80–82
investment: of money, 9, 21–22; of time, 6, 45, 64

journal, for gratitude, 115

keystone habit, 66–67
Kondo, Marie: *The Life-Changing Magic of Tidying Up* by, 51–52
Kruse, Kevin, 65

leaning in, to stress, 89–90
Lee, Ivy, 46

leverage your time, 63
Lewis, Michael: *Moneyball* by, 59–60
The Life-Changing Magic of Tidying Up (Kondo), 51–52
life preserver, for predisposing triggers, 98–99

machine readable text, 53
Making Habits, Breaking Habits (Dean), 65
Maltz, Maxwell, 67
management *vs.* leadership, 139
Mary Poppins, 68
massage: for stress management, 106–107; therapist for, 109
massage therapist, 109
meditation, 126; falsehoods about, 104; massage as, 107; schools of, 104–105; Shamatha, 104–106, *105*; for stress management, 69, 88, 101, 103–06
meetings: as black hole of time, 62–63; efficiency related to, 5; inventorying, 62; stress from, 86–87, 97–98
mental model, for precipitating triggers, 100
mental shift, as coping mechanism, 126–27
mental vacation: as coping mechanism, 119–20; as "happy place," 120
metaphors, 3; black holes of time as, 61; of personal energy cycle, 25–28, *26*, *27*, *28*; rocks, pebbles, and sand as, 10–12, *11*, 17, 40
metta mindfulness, exercises for, 113–15
Miller, Arthur, 55
mindfulness meditation. *See* meditation
Mindset (Dweck), 90–91
money: budgeting, 9–12; investment of, 9, 21–22; time contrasted with, 7–10, 19–22
Moneyball (Lewis), 59–60
Money Ball Principle, 59–60
money management *vs.* time management, 7–10

multitasking, lacking efficiency, 38
muscles, stretching of, 108–109, *109*
music: relaxing sounds as, 117; for stress management, 116–17

nexus of resources, 20–24, *21*; energy level in, 25

obstacles: to efficiency, 4–5, 47–48; of habits, 67; to time management, 41
O'Connor, Richard: *Rewire* by, 65
OHIO Method, 48–51
One-at-a-Time System, for to-do lists, 45–46
one-touch method, 68
Only Handle It Once. See OHIO Method
opportunity cost *vs.* actual cost, 24
organization: of e-mail, 49–50; of to-do list, 43–44; of workspace, 51, 53, 134
origins, of stress, 73, 83
outcomes, driving goals, 58
outsourcing, of tasks, 22–24
overt *vs.* covert: precipitating triggers and, 100; predisposing triggers and, 96–97
Oxford English Dictionary, 83

Paired Comparisons System, for to-do lists, 44–45
patterns: in energy cycle, 34; in time log, 37
PDF. *See* Adobe Portable Document Format
peaks and valleys, of energy cycle, 30, 38
people, in nexus of resources, 20, *21*, 48–49
performance, stress influencing, 76–77, *77*
perpetual unresolved stress, 74
phone time, time clustering for, 40
plan, for stress management, 131–32
the plateau (metaphor), 27, *27*, 39
poses, yoga, 110–12, *111–12*
positive mood, of academic leaders, 139–40

power, of prayer, 114
The Power of Habit (Duhigg), 65–67
PowerPoint, 21–23
prayer: power of, 114; for stress management, 113–15
pre-Bötzinger complex, 102–103
precipitating triggers, *81*, 81–82, 93, *94*; control over, 93, 95–96, 99–100; mental model for, 100
predisposing triggers, *81*, 81–82, 93, *94*; cognitive restructuring of, 97–98; control over, 93, 94–95, 96–99; life preserver for, 98–99
prerequisites, for stress management: diet, exercise, sleep as, 79–80, 135–36
prevention, of time waste, 9–10, 47, 49
principles, of to-do list, 42–46
priorities: of academic leadership, 5, 44; for time management, 9–10; values guiding, 9, 134, 136
prioritization: within energy cycle, 28–30, 34; of goals, 12, 35, 134; of resources, 20; of tasks, 5, 14–15, 16–17, 38, 40, 44–45
proactivity: for *stress leadership*, 96; of work, 40
project management, 43
projects: as series of tasks, 43, 88; tasks *vs.*, *42*, 42–43, 57
public speaking, 99
punch list, for holistic approach, 137

quality, of work, 30–31, 34, 38, 76
quality time, in schedule, 38–40
quiet hours, time clustering for, 39

redirection, of energy, 33–34, 134–35
reduction, of stress, 93–100
relaxation: serene moment for, 121–22; for stress management, 94–95, 102–07
relaxing sounds, 117
reprogramming habits, 65–67; cue, routine, reward and, 66, 68

resources: of academic leadership, 19–24, 48, 126, 131; nexus of, 20–24, *21*; prioritization of, 20
retention rate, 56–57, 58
Rewire (O'Connor), 65
rocks, pebbles, and sand (metaphor), 10–12, *11*, 17, 40
role models, academic leaders as, 140
rounds, task clustering, 39

schedule: for documents, 49, 51; energy cycle and, 28, 30–31, 38–39; stakeholders and, 39; task clustering of, 38–40; of tasks, 10, 12, 16–17, 43, 51; for to-do list, 43–44, 46
scheduling your priorities, 43
Schmich, Mary, 90
schools: of meditation, 104–105; of yoga, 109–10
Schwab, Charles M., 46
secularism, in prayer, 113–15
Selye, Hans, 83, 84–85, 87, 91
serene moment/refuge, 125; as coping mechanism, 120–22, 126; creating, 122; workspace as, 120–21
services, on Internet, 21–22
Seven Habits of Highly Effective People (Covey), 14, 14–15, 65
Shamatha meditation, 104–106, *105*
simple *vs.* complex, habits, 67
the skier (metaphor), *26*, 26–27, 38
sleep, for stress management, 79–80, 135–36
Smarter, Faster, Better (Duhigg), 65
SMARTER Goals, 58, *59*, 60
SMART Goals, 55–58, *56*, 60
smartphone app: for deep breathing, 103; for time log, 37–38; for to-do list, 43–44
sorting, documents, 50–51
space, in nexus of resources, 20, *21*
Specific, Measurable, Achievable, Responsible, Time-Related. *See* SMART Goals
Specific, Measurable, Achievable, Responsible, Time-Related,

Enthusiasm, Rewards. *See* SMARTER Goals
stakeholders: demands of, 4, 47; energy and, 28, 31–33; engagement of, 58; schedule and, 39
stamina, for workload, 34
Stanford University School of Medicine, 102
Star Wars, 116
sticky notes, for to-do list, 43–44
strategic nonresponse: *Bless and Release* as, 123; as coping mechanism, 122–23, 126
stress: benefits of, 76–77, 88; control and safety in, 85–87; coping mechanisms for, 119–26; cortisol effect of, 74, 83; deadlines causing, 73, 76, 81; enjoyment of, 84–87, 89–90; fight-or-flight response to, 73–74; good *vs.* bad, 76–79; inventorying, *74–75,* 74–76, 77–79, *78,* 80–82; leaning in to, 89–90; meetings causing, 86–87, 97–98; origins of, 73, 83; performance influenced by, 76–77, *77;* tolerance for, 78–79, 82, 91; transforming, 87–88, 89–90, 91, 101; triggers of, 80–82, *81,* 83–85, 89, 93, 131; venting, 132
stress leadership, 96, 139–40
stress levels, exercises for, *74–75,* 74–76, 77–79, *78*
stress management: growth mind-set for, 87, 90–91; holistic approach to, 80, 82, 118, 127, 131, 135, *136;* humor for, 133; intentions for, 80; plan for, 131–32; prerequisites for, 79–80; relaxation and, 94–95, 102–107; strategy for, *136;* techniques for, 82, 101–18; through writing, 132. *See also* specific topics
stretching, exercises: of muscles, 108–109, *109;* for stress management, 108–109; yoga contrasted with, 110
structure, for prayer, 113
student recruiting, 3–4

systems, for to-do list, 44–46

TaskRabbit, 22
tasks: as black holes of time, 61; clustering, 38–40; deadline-driven, 13–15, 43; eliminating, 16, 35; energy cycle linked to, 28, *29,* 30–31, 35, 38; enjoying, 68–69; outsourcing, 22–24; prioritizing, 5, 14–15, 16–17, 38, 40, 44–45; projects broken into, 43, 88; projects *vs.,* *42,* 42–43, 57; scheduling, 10, 12, 16–17, 43, 51; values driving, 14, 134
technology, in nexus of resources, 20, *21*
The Third Man, 76
thriving on busy, 67–68, 139
tidiness, commitment to, 51–52
time: in academic year, 4–5; budgeting, 7–10; contrasted with money, 7–10, 19–22; goals for managing, 5–6; investment of, 6, 45, 64; *leveraging,* 63. *See also* black holes of time; time management
time and money, 19; as resources, 20; value of, 22–23
time log: creation of, 36–38; efficiency through, 35–36, *36–37,* 38; energy level and, 37; smartphone app for, 37–38; for time management, 35–38
time management: budget for, 6, 9–12; energy cycle and, 28–34, 67; holistic approach to, 127, 135, *136;* money management *vs.,* 7–10; priorities for, 9–10; strategy of, *136;* time log for, 35–38; to-do list for, 41–46; during travel, 22; waste contrasted with, 3, 7, 9–10, 36, 41
"time puddles and lakes," 9–10, 51
to-do list: benefits of, 41, 43; Paired Comparisons System for, 44–45; smartphone app/sticky notes for, 43–44; systems for, 44–46; tasks *vs.* projects in, 42–43; for time management, 41–46

tolerance, for stress, 78–79, 82, 91
the trampoline (metaphor), 27, *28*, 38
transformation, of stress, 87–88, 89–90, 91, 101
travel, time management and, 22
triggers, of stress, 80–82, *81*, 83–85, 131; avoiding, 93, 96, 101; control over, 93–100; fear and, 89, 96–97; precipitating and predisposing, *81*, 81–82, 93, *94*, 94–100; types of, *94*
Twain, Mark, 97
types, of triggers, *94*

Ultradian Rhythms, 25
UpWork, 22
urgent *vs.* important, *13*, 43, 45, 66–67, 134–36; efficiency and, 17; exercises for, 15–16

value: of resources, 20; of time and money, 22–23

values: as driver of tasks, 14, 134; priorities guided by, 9, 134, 136
ventilation, of stress, 132
virtual assistance, 21

waste, of time, 3, 7, 36, 41; preventing, 9–10, 47, 49
Williams, John, 116
work: breaks from, 121, 125; engagement with, 34, 135–36; proactive contrasted with reactive, 40; quality of, 30–31, 34, 38, 76
workload: of academic leadership, 3–4, 115; stamina for, 34
workspace: organizing, 51, 53, 134; as serene refuge, 120–21
writing, for stress management, 132

yoga: poses for, 110–12, *111–12*; schools of, 109–10; for stress management, 109–12
YouTube, 112

About the Author

Jeffrey L. Buller, current director of leadership and professional development at Florida Atlantic University, has served in administrative positions ranging from department chair to vice president for academic affairs at four very different institutions: Loras College, Georgia Southern University, Mary Baldwin College, and Florida Atlantic University. He is the author of more than a dozen books on higher education administration, a textbook for first-year college students, and a book of essays on the music dramas of Richard Wagner. Dr. Buller has also written numerous articles on Greek and Latin literature, nineteenth- and twentieth-century opera, and college administration. From 2003 to 2005, he served as the principal English-language lecturer at the International Wagner Festival in Bayreuth, Germany. More recently, he has been active as a consultant to the Ministry of Education in Saudi Arabia, where he is assisting with the creation of a kingdom-wide academic leadership center. Along with Robert E. Cipriano, Dr. Buller is a senior partner in ATLAS: Academic Training, Leadership, & Assessment Services, through which he has presented numerous workshops on college administration, including sessions on time management and stress management for academic leaders.

www.ingramcontent.com/pod-product-compliance
Lightning Source LLC
Chambersburg PA
CBHW021844220426
43663CB00005B/396